PRECEPTS FOR LIVING®

PASTOR'S EDITION
SERMON OUTLINES

UMI

THE UMI ANNUAL COMMENTARY 2022–2023

PRECEPTS FOR LIVING®

PASTOR'S EDITION

MISSION STATEMENT

We are called
of God to create, produce, and distribute
quality Christian education products;
to deliver exemplary customer service;
and to provide quality Christian
educational services, which will empower
God's people, especially within the Black
community, to evangelize, disciple,
and equip people for serving Christ,
His kingdom, and church.

UMI

PRECEPTS FOR LIVING® 2022–2023
PASTOR'S EDITION
VOLUME 16
UMI (URBAN MINISTRIES, INC.)

Melvin Banks Sr., LittD, Founder

C. Jeffrey Wright, JD, CEO

Unless otherwise indicated, Scripture quotations are taken from the King James Version.

ISBN-13: 978-1-68353-855-4

Publisher: UMI (Urban Ministries, Inc.), Chicago, IL 60643.

To place an order, call us at
1-800-860-8642 or visit our website at www.urbanministries.com

UMI

Dear Pastor,

Is it your desire to see the people of God increase in their knowledge of God's Will, love God deeply, and follow God more faithfully? Certainly you will say "yes" because this is the drumbeat of your heart as a pastor!

It is also why UMI exists. God impressed Hosea 4:6 upon me as a boy in Birmingham, Alabama. The truth of that text resulted in my pioneering the establishment of UMI. Hosea 4:6 (NKJV) still rings true today:

"My people are destroyed for lack of knowledge."

This is also why we produce a *Precepts For Living*® Pastor's Edition. We want you to encourage your entire congregation—not just the Sunday School crowd!—to make Bible study a priority during the week. Whether at Sunday School, midweek Bible study, another small group gathering, or family devotions, God's people profit from regular exposure to the Word.

We envision this *Precepts For Living*® Pastor's Edition being used along with the *Precepts For Living*® Annual Commentary. The sermons in this volume correlate with the Bible studies in *Precepts For Living*®. That way your sermons can be reinforced by Bible studies in Sunday School or other small groups. In this edition, we anticipate that you will appreciate these sermons presented as outlines and full texts. Additionally, we have included a sampling of sermons for special occasions. Even if you choose to develop your own sermon from the weekly Bible text, we believe this edition will prove invaluable and will certainly be a catalyst for your preaching.

You will be amazed and delighted at the impact this material will make on your entire congregation. Your church will study a Bible passage and then hear you preach on the same theme or related Bible text.

So enjoy *Precepts For Living*® Pastor's Edition and consider preaching one or more sermons based on the themes or texts. Let us know the result it makes in your congregation.

Sincerely,

Melvin E. Banks Sr., LittD

(October 15, 1934 - February 13, 2021)

PRECEPTS FOR LIVING®

PASTOR'S EDITION

To maximize your entire congregation's biblical learning experience, this resource will help you correlate your sermons with companion Bible studies in the *Precepts For Living®, Annual Commentary*. The continuity between the sermons and the *Precepts* lessons will give further insight into the God-intended meaning of the Scriptures so that your Bible students can successfully understand the principles taught and apply them to their daily living. There are outlines for topical use as well.

LESSON SERMONS

Kindling Wood—Sermon Starters

Kindling Wood, prepared by the Rev. Cheryl Price, Ph.D., and the Rev. William Martin, presents selected sermon titles, main character(s), and Scripture references. This year we added three features. We highlighted what was happening in the text, a comment or question to spark ideas during your sermon preparation, and suggestions for a children's sermon or talk time.

1. Unchain My Heart
David—David needed to repent and receive God into his heart. For what things do we need to repent and surrender our hearts over to God? (Psalm 51:1–10)

2. Someone Who Cares
David—David needs deliverance from his mighty enemies. He feels powerless and alone. Being alone with no one to help you is scary and painful. What is our general response in this situation and to whom do we turn for help? (Psalm 142:4)

3. A Cure for Heart Problems
Twelve Disciples—Jesus indicates to the disciples that His death on the Cross is near and that salvation for all will come because of His death and Resurrection. How do we respond when we hear what we do not want to hear or accept? (John 14:1)

4. Now I Know Why
Paul—Paul explains to believers that even when they suffer, they cannot be separated from the love of Christ. God's love is stronger than anything we could ever endure, regardless of the situation. (Romans 8:36)

5. An Inside Job or The Kiss of a Betrayer
Jesus and Judas—Recall the kiss Jesus receives from Judas in the Garden of Gethsemane. Sometimes our closest friends or family members will do us harm. How should we respond? (Matthew 26:47–56)

6. Can You Hear Me Now?
Habakkuk—Habakkuk's first complaint to God questioned why evil happens and justice does not prevail. Why do bad things happen to believers and nonbelievers go free? (Habakkuk 1:1–4)

7. God's Strange Response
God—God responds to Habakkuk's first complaint by detailing how Israel's punishment will be the Babylonians overtaking them. Complaining to God may require us to hear things we do not want to hear. (Habakkuk 1:5–11)

8. A Midnight Cry At Noon Day
Jesus—Jesus cries out from the Cross that He (His Spirit) is coming home to God and dies. Jesus' cries are a victory for us. (Luke 23:44–49)

9. Why God Can't Sleep
God—Examine the pilgrimage song of the faithful who have the assurance that God is watching over them. What would happen if God slept when you needed Him? (Psalm 121)

10. The Testimony of a Blind Man
Bartimaeus—Jesus and the disciples leave the new city of Jericho and find Bartimaeus, who was blind, sitting by the roadside shouting for Jesus' attention. Jesus doesn't mind if we call out His name when we need help. (Mark 10:46–52)

11. What's In Your Hand? (Use What You've Got!)
Moses—God instructs Moses to use the staff in his hand as a sign to deliver the enslaved people from the Red Sea in front of them and Pharaoh's army quickly approaching them from behind. What's in your hand or before you that God wants you to use for God's glory and to change your life or the lives of others? (Exodus 14:10–18)

12. An Angry Woman's Revenge (Elijah on the Run)
Elijah—After the Mount Carmel experience, Elijah runs away from Queen Jezebel because he is afraid for his life. Who or what are you afraid of? (I Kings 19:1–5)

13. The Showdown Between Paul and Barnabas
Paul and Barnabas—Paul and Barnabas sharply disagree and argue about John Mark traveling with them on their next mission trip. Have you ever argued with another Christian to the point where you stop speaking to one another? (Acts 15:36–41)

14. Forgiveness and Reconciliation
Paul and Barnabas—Paul and Barnabas forgive and reconcile with one another after arguing over John Mark. Forgiveness and reconciliation can take time, even for those who know better. (1 Corinthians 9:6 or Colossians 4:10)

Paul and Mark—Paul and Mark forgive each other and reconcile. Sometimes maturity on both sides and being apart can help some relationships grow in the way that God would like. (2 Timothy 4:11)

15. From Leftovers to Love
Naomi and Ruth—Naomi and Ruth were widows and destitute. Ruth traveled with Naomi to see if her relative, Boaz, would provide refuge for them and a love story evolves. It is good to have a Naomi (or Ned) in your life to help you find and keep your Boaz (or Bonita). (Ruth 2:17–23)

16. A Costly Mistake
Esau and Jacob—Esau, a hunter, returned home starving. His younger brother Jacob was cooking and refused to give Esau food until Esau sold him his birthright. When we do not value who we are and the rights that come with it, we may sell or give away our future joys and possibilities. (Genesis 25:29–34)

17. A Parent's Pain
Esau—Esau's marriage to two Hittite women grieved both of his parents. How do you respond when your children's actions hurt your heart? (Genesis 26:34-35)

18. The Lost and Found Department (Parables by Jesus)
a) The Lost Sheep—The rejoicing in heaven over one sinner repenting is compared to the rejoicing found over righteous people that do not need to repent. People are like sheep and need a shepherd to advocate for and love them when they are lost. (John 15:1–7)

b) The Lost Coin—Rejoicing over a sinner who repents is great in heaven and is compared to the rejoicing over a woman who lost a coin and found it. (John 15:8–10)

c) The Prodigal Son—The younger son leaves home with his inheritance money, but loses the money and his identity through foolish choices. He returns home, but his older brother is angry because of their father's response. Jealousy and an unclear perception of the whole picture keeps us from celebrating the blessings of others. (John 15:25–31)

Children's Sermon Ideas

1. Big Catch of the Day: Prayer!

Acts 13:1–5

Bring in various items that are used for fishing: net, fishing pole, bait, bucket, toy fish, and packs of gummy worms to give to children afterward. Invite children to learn about the various items. You may want to ask if anyone has ever gone fishing. Have children use the fishing pole to catch fish in the bucket. Have one fish in the bucket with the word "prayer" written on it. Once a child has hooked out the fish with the word "prayer," talk about how we sometimes find ourselves looking or fishing for things, but we forget to ask God for help. Remind them that prayer is a way we can stay connected to God and ask Him to aid us when we need Him.

*2. Yelling is a Good Thing (Safety Talk with Children)

Violent acts against children, from bullying to kidnapping, continues to be a problem within our schools, communities, and even in church. During a children's sermon time, have a discussion about helping children protect themselves from people who want to harm them.

Here are a few suggestions that you may want to consider:

1) Have a police officer or community safety advocate talk with children about what to do if they feel threatened or if someone is hurting them.

2) Remind children to be wary of some adults who may try to hurt them and those who may lure them into danger by asking for directions if they want candy, or to see a puppy to lure them away.

3) Encourage children to scream if someone grabs or tries to kidnap them with phrases such as "Stop," "You are not my mother/father," "Help," or "Let me go!" Kicking, screaming, and shouting are OK. Ask the police or maybe some church members to role-play to reinforce these actions.

3. Find the Hidden Coin

John 15:8–10

Gather children together and let them know that today the discussion will be on finding something. Hide a dollar coin or quarter in one of your hands or give the coin to an adult, who will help you later in the sermon. Tell the parable that Jesus shares about the lost coin and the woman searching to find it and how much joy is in heaven when we repent or change our ways to do what God wants us to do.

Tell the group, "Let's see if we can 'appreciate' the rejoicing in heaven and how the woman felt when she found her lost coin. Ask two adults to assist you. Make a huddle or discuss beforehand what will happen. Then each of you will hold out a balled up fist so two or three children can decide which hand has the coin. Tell everyone to shout as loud as they can to celebrate when one child finds the coin.

*adpated from a children's sermon by Pastor Leslie Braxton, New Beginnings Church in Reston, Va.

Contributors

Elder George Akins is senior pastor at Refuge Temple Church of God in Christ, Englewood, New Jersey, and superintendent of Sunday School, New Garden State Jurisdiction, Church of God in Christ, Inc.

Vincent Bacote, Ph.D., is the director of the Center for Applied Christian Ethics and an associate professor of theology at Wheaton College in Wheaton, Illinois and a previous Senior Editor of Precepts for Living.

Dr. Melvin E. Banks, Sr., LittD, was the founder and chairman of Urban Ministries, Inc. (UMI). Under his direction, UMI grew to be one of the leading publishers of Christian education resources for churches in the African American community, serving nearly 100,000 teachers with Sunday School and Vacation Bible School materials. He was a graduate of Moody Bible Institute and the Wheaton College Graduate School.

Brian Bantum, PhD, is an assistant professor of theology at Seattle Pacific University in Seattle, Washington.

Tawanna Boyd is pastor of St. Phillip C.M.E. Church in Cusseta, Georgia.

Kevin Hrebik is a chaplain and president of Hope Behind the Bars and owner of The Paper Whisperer in Houston, Texas.

Moussa Coulibaly received his PhD in theological education from Trinity International University in Deerfield, Illinois. He is currently the executive director of Restoration Ministries in Burkina Faso, a nation located inland in West Africa. This ministry has four primary areas: Elim Bible Institute, five elementary schools with more than 1,600 students, church planting (more than 20 new churches since 2000), and a ministry to orphans and AIDS widows.

Richard Gray, PhD, is professor of Leadership and Christian Ministries at Asbury Theological Seminary in Wilmore, Kentucky.

Aaron O. Howard is currently completing a PhD in religion at Vanderbilt University in Nashville, Tennessee. He is a Fund for Theological Education Doctoral Fellow and an ordained elder in the Church of God in Christ.

Matthew C. Jones is a native of Los Angeles, where he serves as lead pastor of Del Rey Church and teaching assistant of apologetics at Biola University in La Mirada, California.

Contributors

William Martin is part of the ministerial and educational team at True Vine Missionary Baptist Church in Chicago, Ill. Rev. Martin works with youth in the sports program in the Chicago Public Schools. He previously served as the Associate Director of Church Relations at UMI (Urban Ministries, Inc.).

Rev. Robert J. Morgan is pastor of the Donelson Fellowship in Nashville, Tennessee.

Rev. Ronald Clifton Potter is resident scholar of Christian studies and Contemporary Culture at Ekklesia School of Ministry & Theology in Jackson, Miss. He also teaches religion and philosophy at Hinds Community College in Raymond, Mississippi.

Rev. Cheryl Price, PhD, is an ordained Baptist minister, scholar, and publisher. She was previously the vice president of editorial at UMI (Urban Ministries, Inc.).

James Rawdon is a speaker, writer, and former pastor from Lee's Summit, Mo.

Adriana Rivera, MDiv, of East Chicago, Indiana, was a developmental editor with UMI (Urban Ministries, Inc.). She is pursuing doctoral studies in Christian Education and Congregational Studies at Garrett-Evangelical Theological Seminary in Evanston, Illinois. She is a former 7th grade English Language Arts and Sunday School teacher.

Sharon Smith, JD, is an ordained itinerant elder of the African Methodist Episcopal Church. She received her Juris Doctorate from the University of Maryland School of Law and a master of divinity degree from the Interdenominational Theological Center in Atlanta, Georgia. Her area of concentration is biblical studies, specifically biblical law.

Rev. Sylvester Warsaw, Jr. is outreach pastor at First Baptist Church El Cajon in El Cajon, California.

Sermon Evaluation Form

At Urban Ministries, Inc., we strive to provide resources that assist in developing and training students, pastors, and preachers to write and deliver sermons that display

- Faithfulness to Scripture
- Concern for the World
- Authenticity from the Messenger
- and Transformative Power

We created this sermon evaluation to serve as a tool for you to assess a given sermon, whether it be yours, a colleague's, or a student's. This tool can be utilized to evaluate either a written or preached sermon.

Ratings: 1 - Outstanding; 2 - Great; 3 - Good; 4 - Satisfactory; 5 - Unsatisfactory

Preacher's Name

____

Sermon Title

____

Name of Church

____

Scripture Passage

____

Date

____

---

1. Faithfulness to Scripture

The sermons should be faithful to the words of the text and should provide evidence of close engagement with the main points and issues of it. The sermons should cohere to the larger narrative of God's revelation in Scripture.

Ratings: 1 - Outstanding; 2 - Great; 3 - Good; 4 - Satisfactory; 5 - Unsatisfactory

Section 1

The sermon content demonstrated faithful engagement with Scripture.

1 2 3 4 5

The sermon content helped you understand the Scripture.

1 2 3 4 5

The sermon content illuminated God's presence in the text.

1 2 3 4 5

The sermon content connected the text to God's presence and action in the larger biblical narrative.

1 2 3 4 5

Section 2

Was a main point in the text clearly presented in the sermon? If so, please state your understanding of the main point based on the sermon:

2. Concern for World (Contextual)

The sermon should connect God's presence and activity in the text to the issues in today's world. The sermon should address how the message can be understood in the light of the major social and personal challenges of the listeners.

Ratings: 1 - Outstanding; 2 - Great; 3 - Good; 4 - Satisfactory; 5 - Unsatisfactory

Section 1

The sermon content demonstrated an awareness of today's major issues.

1 2 3 4 5

The sermon content showed a clear connection from the message of the text to a particular problem or issue in the world.

1 2 3 4 5

The sermon content drew appropriate and useful analogies between the biblical world and contemporary society/culture.

1 2 3 4 5

You felt empowered by the sermon to address the concerns in the world or your community.

1 2 3 4 5

Section 2

Please list an example or two of how the sermon resonated with the social context(s) of today's world.

3. Authenticity of the Messenger

The writer or preacher of the sermon should demonstrate that the message in Scripture has convicted him or her at a personal level. Thus, personal engagement and thoughtfulness should be evident in the sermon, with the preacher conveying an authentic voice.

Ratings: 1 - Outstanding; 2 - Great; 3 - Good; 4 - Satisfactory; 5 - Unsatisfactory

Section 1

The preacher approached the text in a genuine way.

1 2 3 4 5

A consistent voice or perspective was presented in an authentic way.

1 2 3 4 5

The preacher conveyed personal engagement and deep thoughtfulness on the text.

1 2 3 4 5

The preacher demonstrated conviction and passion for the topic and text.

1 2 3 4 5

Section 2

Please elaborate on the sense of authenticity you received from the preacher. What confirmed that the messenger was engaged and connected to the text?

4. Transformative Power

The sermons should challenge, encourage, and strengthen your congregation in their attempts to become faithful disciples of Jesus. Message points should use illustrations or scenarios that are relevant and meet listeners' experiences in their daily living. The explication of the text should be easy to apply to any number of situations.

Ratings: 1 - Outstanding; 2 - Great; 3 - Good; 4 - Satisfactory; 5 - Unsatisfactory

Section 1

The sermon content was relevant for challenging, encouraging, and strengthening believers in their journey of Christian discipleship.

1 2 3 4 5

The sermon content lends itself to transformational living for believers.

1 2 3 4 5

The sermons addressed a specific area of life that relates to faithfully living as a believer.

1 2 3 4 5

The sermons contained the potential to be life-changing for a wide range of listeners.

1 2 3 4 5

Section 2

Please comment briefly on the potential for transformative power of the sermon.

5. Sermon Delivery

If applicable, evaluate the preacher on his or her delivery of the given sermon using the following:

Ratings: 1 - Outstanding; 2 - Great; 3 - Good; 4 - Satisfactory; 5 - Unsatisfactory

Section 1

The preacher held a posture and used body language that was fitting for the content of the message.

1 2 3 4 5

The preacher delivered the sermon in a clear and understandable tone of voice, and showed variation at appropriate points to place emphasis.

1 2 3 4 5

The preacher conveyed a strong sense of confidence in the message and the delivery.

1 2 3 4 5

The preacher effectively connected to the congregation with consistent eye-contact.

1 2 3 4 5

The preacher showed a deep level of engagement with the message by not simply reading but making it come alive.

1 2 3 4 5

Section 2

Please comment on the strengths and weaknesses you noticed in the delivery of the sermon.

Drawing Near

By Elder Aaron O. Howard

Lesson Theme	Unit Theme	Scripture
Faith Calls for Perseverance	A Living Faith	Hebrews 10:19–31

INTRODUCTION

In the Old Testament, people sometimes had a precarious relationship with God. Fearing judgment, they rarely encountered Him as a friend. Some saw Him a distant ruler who demanded they keep many burdensome laws. The death and resurrection of Christ changed this dynamic, resulting in a monumental impact on our relationships with God and each other. The author of Hebrews describes for us our ability to enter the presence of God without guilt or shame.

MESSAGE POINTS

Message Point 1: Draw Near to God with Confidence (Hebrews 10:19–22)

God is transcendent, meaning He is above and beyond human categories of time and space. God is not bound by the laws of physics that govern human existence, and He far surpasses our modes of reasoning and understanding (Isaiah 55:8–9). It would seem impossible to draw near to God considering the realities of human existence do not compare to the infinite ways of God. However, the author lets us know that God is also immanent, meaning God allows us to fellowship with Him and experience His love through encounters that are concrete and real.

God invites us to draw near to Him with confidence, meaning we should not cower in fear at the thought of God's might and strength. We should reach toward Him because He has demonstrated His great love for us. We can feel the presence of God and know that although He is beyond this world, He also exists in this world through His relationship with us.

Jesus' sacrifice reconciles us to God because Jesus' flesh was torn, just like the veil in the temple. This means we do not have to stand outside of the presence of God like those who were not High Priests in the times of the Old Testament. Instead, all who believe have access to the presence of God through the sacrifice of Jesus Christ. The torn veil symbolizes the complete removal of all obstacles to intimacy with the Lord. We are completely forgiven and can come to God in faith, knowing that He cares for us and loves us.

Message Point 2: Draw Near to One Another (Hebrews 10:23–25)

Faith without works is dead (James 2:17). We demonstrate our love for God by following His commandments (John 14:15). One of God's commandments to us is that we love one another. How can we say we love God whom we have not seen if we cannot love our brothers and sisters in the faith with whom we regularly interact (I John 4:20)? The author provides three ways for showing this love:

The author admonishes believers to collectively hold on to our faith. When trials come, it is easy for us to become overly individualistic and to focus on ourselves. However, we must gain strength from fellow believers, and they too can hold onto their faith by gaining strength from us. We should always proclaim and reiterate the confession of our hope to one another. Our hope in Christ should be at the forefront of our conversations, and it should be a continual source of encouragement for the church community.

We should motivate others to show love through their deeds. Instead of gossiping or becoming involved in conversations that denigrate others, we should suggest ways that others can be blessed. For example, we can encourage others to pray for fellow church members, or we can develop ways of providing for the needs of less fortunate church members. In one church, the women's group adopted a less fortunate family and collected donations so that the children of this family could have Christmas gifts. This is love in action.

We should not neglect our responsibility to attend church regularly. As society becomes more immoral and as the temptations of the enemy grow stronger, we need to gain strength and encouragement from solidarity within the body of Christ. Just as a predator hunts the animals that stray from the herd, we become easy targets for the enemy when we refrain from the worship and fellowship that occur when we faithfully attend church.

Message Point 3: Draw Near to Avoid Returning to a Life of Sin (Hebrews 10:26–31)

Some people, after experiencing the grace and love of God, still return to a life of sin and reject Jesus Christ. For these people, God promises His wrath on the Day of Judgment. Although grace is free, it is not cheap, and we should treat God's grace as a valuable, priceless jewel (Matthew 13:45–46). While we are not perfect, we should strive to live a sanctified life, and if we sin, we should immediately repent (1 John 2:1). To continually sin without embracing repentance demonstrates pride and hostility to spiritual things. This lack of humility insults the Spirit of God and eventually results in God's wrath. However, God's grace is always there to forgive us if we sincerely turn away from evil.

THAT'LL PREACH

Consider Esther's experience of having to go before the king (Esther 5). Even though the king was her husband, she was risking her life to come before him without being called. But she knew she had to stand up for her people. The risk paid off as the king accepted her and granted her request. Isn't it amazing that, thanks to the sacrifice of Jesus, we can come boldly before God's throne? We don't have to fear being rejected by the King of Kings (1 Timothy 6:15), who is also the Bridegroom of the Church (John 3:29). We can share our concerns for our people and trust that God will move because of God's great love for us.

CONCLUSION

Jesus' great sacrifice enables us to come to God boldly and with confidence. This is not a rash boldness that is arrogant, but it refers to the sense that we are secure and safe in the love of God. However, we also understand that our participation in this grace coincides with our diligent efforts to serve God through our worship, acts of loving others, and faithfulness to the principles and teachings of Christ. By drawing near to Christ and each other, we are saved from the judgment to come.

Faith is Assurance

By Elder Aaron O. Howard

Lesson Theme	Unit Theme	Scripture
Faith Is Assurance	A Living Faith	Hebrews 11:1–3, 6; Psalm 46:1–3, 8–11

INTRODUCTION

Our society values observable evidence as the primary criterion for belief. As science becomes more precise in its discoveries, humanity becomes more dependent on empirical evidence—that which can be observed and tested through experimentation—for ascertaining truth. For example, DNA evidence has set free many criminals who were convicted decades earlier because it provides observable and reliable evidence for whether a person was involved in a crime. However, the author in our text shows that faith values and believes in what is not seen and that it is superior to evidence which relies on observable phenomena alone.

Furthermore, faith is more than mental assent or cognitive belief. It extends to our actions. I have faith that a chair will support my weight only if I sit down on it. Therefore, we show that we have faith in God when we trust in Him as our strength and refuge.

MESSAGE POINTS

Message Point 1: Faith Believes in the Unseen (Hebrews 11:1–3, 6)

There are spiritual realities that cannot be seen with the natural eye including God Himself, Satan, Heaven, and Hell. The only reliable access that we have to this spiritual domain is through the Word of God. We did not see Jesus rise from the dead, but because the Word of God testifies that He rose, we believe it. We have not yet experienced the Second Coming of Jesus Christ, but because the Word of God promises it, we believe it. We have assurance and confidence that what the Lord promises us through His Word has happened, is happening, and will happen. Just like DNA is the evidence to convict or acquit a criminal, faith is our evidence that the things that we cannot see exist in the way that God describes them. Even what we see, the physical world, was made from that which is unseen, the Word of God. If God's Word is sufficient to create the world, then we can trust in Him wholeheartedly.

Without this faith in God, we cannot please Him. It is not through our intelligence, ability, or accomplishments that we ultimately please the Lord, but we please Him by believing that He exists and having confidence in His loving and forgiving nature. He rewards us with the gift of salvation when we humbly cry out for mercy and repentance through faith.

Message Point 2: Faith Trusts God in Times of Trouble (Psalm 46:1–3)

Trials and tribulations are endemic to human existence. It is not a matter of if we will experience them but simply a matter of when. The psalmist reminds us that in the midst of turmoil and chaos, our faith should cause us to depend on God as our strength and refuge. Other people do not have the last word, but God is ultimately in control of our lives and the circumstances surrounding them. In spite of sickness and disease, natural disasters, economic recessions and downturns, family problems, or whatever woes we may encounter, God will protect us, hide us from the storm, and give us strength to stand in the midst of adversity.

Message Point 3: Faith Knows That God is Able (Psalm 46:8–11)

We have faith in God because He has proven His trustworthiness through His mighty acts. Israel had faith in God, and He delivered them from the Egyptians and brought them into the Promised Land. This formative experience enabled them to be continually reminded of God's might and strength when they faced their enemies. In the same way, God has done mighty acts in our lives that should remind us that we can trust Him. While faith believes in the unseen, faith also trusts that God's nature is consistent and that He who delivered us before will also deliver us again. The Lord of Hosts dwells with us and empowers us to overcome whatever obstacles the enemy places in our path. God is our stronghold, and by having faith in Him, we cannot be shaken.

THAT'LL PREACH

Martin Luther King, Jr. once said, "Faith is taking the first step even when you don't see the whole staircase." As we move onwards and upwards in this journey of life, we may feel stuck on a step because we do not know what is coming next. We are unsure if the job, house, or relationship we desire will come to fruition. And based on what we see on the news and experience in our daily lives, it seems like society is taking steps backwards in terms of justice and equality. But by faith, we can take that next step because we trust in the One who built the staircase.

CONCLUSION

Although society tries to exalt reason and opinion above faith, we know through our texts that faith is the highest form of knowing. The philosopher Soren Kierkegaard refuted other philosophers who felt that faith was the beginning of knowledge, and he asserted that faith constitutes ultimate knowledge. We do not adequately know anything until we know God through faith. In Christ, everything finds its fullest meaning (Colossians 1:15–17), and by trusting in Christ alone, we come to know and experience the power of God.

As Christians, we should never feel that faith is subservient to science, technology, or human ingenuity. We must trust in God because only He has the power to sustain us through the trials that will inevitably make an impact on our lives.

NOTES

Winning the Race by Faith

By Aaron O. Howard

Lesson Theme	Unit Theme	Scripture
Faith Is Endurance	A Living Faith	Hebrews 12:1–11

INTRODUCTION

The life of a Christian is more like a marathon than a sprint. The author describes it as a race in which endurance is needed. While speed is the most desired attribute when shorter races are run, long races require the type of stamina that only arises from consistent training, self-sacrifice, and discipline. This arduous training allows one to resist the forces of frustration, doubt, fear, confusion, and weariness that impede the progress of many Christians and cause them to abandon the race. We must keep our eyes on Jesus, for He is the reward that awaits us when we finish our journey.

MESSAGE POINTS

Message Point 1: Rules for Running (Hebrews 12:1–3)

The author reminds us of the many witnesses—whose names and testimonies are mentioned in chapter 11—that successfully finished the Christian race. Their faithfulness to the principles and teachings of Christ reassure us that we can successfully endure by faith. The following three principles will help us finish this race:

We must lay aside everything that hinders and entangles us (v. 1). Marathon runners do not run weighed down by bulky clothing and gadgets. Their clothing is light and minimal. Their bodies are not encumbered by extra weight from unhealthy eating that could slow them down. This allows them to persevere during the later miles when fatigue sets in. The same is true of us as Christians. Those small sins and bad habits that we ignore now will negate our attempts to endure until the end. We must eschew every vestige of sin in our lives by seeking God through prayer, fasting, and Scripture study so that we are not burdened by unnecessary hindrances.

We must fix our eyes on Jesus, who is our perfect example of what it means to endure (v. 2). Runners are motivated by the prize that they receive upon successful completion of a race. Whether that is a gold medal, a sum of money, or the accolades of peers, keeping the prize in mind allows one to train in spite of the pain. By keeping our eyes fixed upon Jesus, who showed us what it means to endure through His death on the Cross, we gain motivation and strength to run vigilantly.

We must understand that there is no glory without suffering (v. 3). Jesus only ascended to the right hand of His Father after He completed His work. Throughout His ministry, He endured the derision and virulence of people who tried to undermine His divine purpose and mission. Just as runners have to endure adverse weather, uneven terrain, and bodily pain, we too will have to endure suffering while running this Christian race. We cannot live godly lives without suffering persecution (2 Timothy 3:12). By meditating on the life of Christ, we are comforted in knowing that a reward awaits us if we do not lose heart (Galatians 6:9).

Message Point 2: Discipline Brings Out the Best in Us (Hebrews 12:4–11)

When we encounter hardship, we often feel that God has abandoned us. To the contrary, the author reminds us that hardship is often God's way of disciplining us like a parent who lovingly corrects their child. God acts like a personal trainer or coach who challenges the athlete to become better, faster, and stronger through a strict regimen characterized by rigorous exercises, difficult drills, an austere diet, and little time for frivolity. God uses hardship to sharpen our spiritual exercises of prayer and Bible study. He allows suffering so we can be tested on whether we are more closely resembling His nature. The discipline and hardship, although painful when we go through it, later leads to a harvest of righteousness and peace if we do not give up (v. 11). God knows exactly how to help us learn the habits and virtues that sustain our endurance. We must submit to His discipline with a joyful heart, knowing that we are being perfected (James 1:2).

THAT'LL PREACH

During the 400-meter semi-finals of the 1992 Summer Olympics in Barcelona, Derek Redmond, a Black British sprinter, tore his hamstring in the middle of the race. Instead of being rushed off the track by medics, he decided to limp and hobble until he completed the lap. When the pain became too much, his father came down from the stands and helped him finish the race. Even though Redmond was technically disqualified from the race, the father-son duo received a standing ovation. We too, have a heavenly Father, who holds us up when we fall, when we are in too much pain to carry on. Our Father will help us finish the race of faith and we will be celebrated with the cheers of the great cloud of witnesses.

CONCLUSION

God equips us with everything we need to successfully finish the Christian race. He gives us grace to endure, and He instructs us through His Word. God tests us with trials and hardship so that we will develop the attributes necessary for successful completion of this race. We must always meditate on Jesus Christ, who went before us as a perfect example of what it means to live a life committed to God's will. He only ascended to glory after enduring the Cross, and we will receive the reward of Christ's eternal presence after we have finished our course.

NOTES

Faith Inspires Gratitude

By Elder Aaron O. Howard

Lesson Theme	Unit Theme	Scripture
Faith Inspires Gratitude	A Living Faith	Hebrews 12:18–29

INTRODUCTION

The New Covenant, inaugurated by the death and resurrection of Jesus Christ is predicated upon grace. It is different than the Mosaic Covenant, which required sacrifices and a multitude of rituals for the absolution of sin. Under the Old Covenant, God's wrath judged sin quickly and the punishment was often severe. Under the New Covenant, however, grace abounds, and our relationship with God is characterized by freedom and joy. We must be careful not to take this grace for granted, assuming that our relationship with God is insignificant or just a tangential part of our lives. We must realize the seriousness of our covenant with God and live our lives with an attitude of thanksgiving and worship.

MESSAGE POINTS

Message Point 1: Description of the Old Covenant (Hebrews 12:18–21)

In these verses, the author describes Israel's relationship with God in the wilderness. The mountain detailed here symbolizes the judgment and wrath associated with the Old Covenant, and the author summarizes the experience of the Israelites when they encountered God in the wilderness of Sinai (Exodus 19:10–25). In this event, God tells Moses to consecrate the people so He can appear to them on Mt. Sinai. God's appearance is not characterized by the people's joy and gladness but by fear and trembling. When God appears the mountain quakes, the trumpet sounds, and smoke emanates from the mountain. The author contrasts this old way of experiencing God with a new way of knowing Him. God's appearance in our midst is no longer a cause for fear and alarm but one for rejoicing.

Message Point 2: Description of the New Covenant (Hebrews 12:22–24)

The author introduces this contrast by describing the New Covenant, where we have come into the dwelling place of God. On Mount Zion, in the heavenly Jerusalem, angels are gathered together, and the blood of Christ speaks of better things than the blood of Abel. Whereas the blood of Abel cried out for the judgment of Cain after he killed his brother, the blood of Christ cries out for mercy and forgiveness on our behalf. The faithful witnesses are gathered here as well, and they are described as the "firstborn" and as the "spirits of the righteous" (v. 23). This city is characterized by joy, something the author communicates by using the Greek word "*panegyric*" to refer to the assembly. In the Greek Old Testament and in secular literature, it refers to a joyous event where there is a festival-like atmosphere. When we come into the presence of God, there is joy (Psalm 16:11)!

Message Point 3: An Admonition to Listen (Hebrews 12:25–29)

With this new covenant comes great responsibility. We are now offered access to the presence of God and the opportunity for joyful and intimate relationship. We cannot forget, however, that our God is holy and that He demands our allegiance. God reminds us that one day, He will not only shake the earth, as He did on Mt. Sinai, but He will also shake the heavens. Heaven and earth will be dissolved, but only the Kingdom of God will remain (Matthew 24:35; 2 Peter 3:10). With this in view, we must respond in gratitude to God because we are inhabitants of the kingdom that cannot be shaken. Our response is to hear the voice of God, obey Him, and to worship Him in reverence.

THAT'LL PREACH

Family reunions are a time of joyful celebration, and a testament of what God has done. Folks from far and wide gather in the city where the family was founded, grew, and developed. Filled with music and the best food, generations are united by love. Imagine the immense joy that will be present in the ultimate family reunion of God's people. Thanks to the New Covenant, instead of cowering in fear, we will worship and celebrate in God's presence in a whole new city. The blood ties of family bring people together for such occasions as reunions, but it is the blood of Christ that brings God's family together.

CONCLUSION

When someone has a position of power over another person, such as a boss or supervisor, that person in authority will often limit the level of intimacy within the relationship. The relationship will most likely remain professional and businesslike, and the two individuals may never become friends. This is because the boss does not want his or her kindness to be mistaken for weakness. God, on the other hand, of infinite power and authority, does the exact opposite. He does not limit the level of friendship and intimacy with Him that we can attain. However, He does recognize the tendency of humans to take advantage of those who are nice and compassionate to them. God warns us not to mistake His grace for permission to be apathetic and complacent regarding our salvation. We are to listen to His voice and always remember to worship Him through reverence, awe, and submission.

NOTES

Faith Requires Mutual Love

By Elder George Akins, Jr.

Lesson Theme	Unit Theme	Scripture
Faith Requires Mutual Love	A Living Faith	Hebrews 13:1–3; 1 Corinthians 13

INTRODUCTION

The design of Christ's offering in giving Himself for humanity is that He may purchase for Himself a redeemed people who are peculiar in their ways toward God and peculiar in their ways towards each other. Different in the social, cultural, and religious context by demonstrating a zeal towards God through good works toward others. The author, after having warned the Hebrews against apostasy, closes his epistle to the Hebrews with recommendations on several excellent social duties. His thoughts were that the believer may have proper fruit of their faith. These duties, according to Paul, are an outward manifestation of an inward transformation. Paul illuminates the inward renewal as the source that produces the evidence of an unfailing, self-sacrificing, spiritual love that does not seek its own recognition.

MESSAGE POINTS

Message Point 1: Brotherly Love Continues (Hebrews 13:1–2)

Charity is a distinctly special manifestation of grace within the Church (Hebrews 6:10; 10:32–34; 12:12, 13). The phrase, "Be not forgetful" implies it was a duty already recognized, but which they might forget to act on (Hebrews 13:3, 7, 16). The enemies of Christianity themselves may have noticed the practice of this virtue among Christians toward Christians and non-Christians. Abraham and Lot are examples of those who have "Entertained angels unawares" (Gen. 18:2; 19:1); the Church is invited to eliminate the natural distrust of strangers. If he or she is a Christian, then the stranger may represent Christ Himself. There is a play on the same Greek word, "Be not forgetful and unaware; let not the duty of hospitality to strangers escape you," meaning that by entertaining strangers, it has escaped the entertainers that they were entertaining angels. Not unconscious and forgetful of the duty, they have unconsciously brought on themselves the blessing.

Message Point 2: Remember Those in Prison (v. 3)

You may have heard the phrase "out of sight, out of mind" but if we are to live out the command to love presented in this passage in our daily lives, we must include those whose sufferings we may not see. In the Roman colonial context, prisoners relied on the kindness of others for their basic needs, including food. Today there are members of our community who continue to be adversely affected by hunger, incarceration, persecution.

Message Point 3: Love in Its Fullest Meaning– True Love to God and Man (1 Corinthians 13)

The absence of love in the presence of glorious gifts is of no account to us or to God. A sharp mind and deep understanding are of no value without a benevolent and charitable heart. Doing good to others without love for God and goodwill to men does no good for us. Prophecies, tongues, and knowledge have their limits. But love goes beyond limts. Paul is cautioning readers to not overvalue these other things at the expense of experiencing and expressing love in its fullest meaning and to its fullest extent.

THAT'LL PREACH

In a 1967 sermon titled, "Where Do We Go From Here?," Martin Luther King, Jr. said, "Power at its best is love implementing the demands of justice, and justice at its best is power correcting everything that stands against love." Today's text reminds us of the power of love and how that power is best expressed when we welcome the stranger. There are those who have become strangers or "alien" among us, including immigrants and those who have been or are currently incarcerated. We are called to show them the love of Christ, a radical love that radiates justice. These "aliens" may very well be the angels talked about in the text.

CONCLUSION

Agape love is clear proof of regeneration and transformation. It is the cornerstone of our faith in Christ. In this beautiful description of the nature and effects of love, Paul attempts to expose the Corinthians in that their conduct had, in many respects, been contrary to the intentions of Christ and His behavior toward the body of believers. Love is an enemy to selfishness; it does not desire or seek its own praise or honor or profit or pleasure. Seek to evaluate the motives behind our individual and organizational behavior as the Church.

NOTES

Stephen's Arrest and Speech

By Elder George Akins, Jr.

Lesson Theme	Unit Theme	Scripture
Stephen's Arrest and Speech	A Living Faith	Acts 6:8–7:2a

INTRODUCTION

People need a bold, perceptive leader to articulate truth in times of uncertainty. Stephen, in the face of opposition, demonstrated the power and wisdom of the Spirit to speak the truth of Christ. Stephen's life and ministry proves the truth of the Gospel. He wrought miracles in the name of Jesus Christ. He did not see himself as someone special, rather, just a servant being diligent and faithful in the discharge of the duties he had been appointed. His faith filled him until there was no room for unbelief or doubt. The value and character of his life and ministry appear to be uncontested in the eyes of both believers and those opposed to the faith, a life is completely consumed by the presenceof God's spirit.

MESSAGE POINTS

Message Point 1: By Faith, the Power of God is Engaged for Us (Acts 6:8)

Stephen's life was a testament of what it meant to be "full of grace and power." By faith, he was emptied of himself and filled with Christ. And by this same faith, he performed great wonders and miracles. Though he was not an apostle, Stephen performed great wonders, the same signs that followed those who believed (Mark 16:17). One does not always have to have an official title to display one's faith and be an example to other believers.

Message Point 2: The Cause of Christianity (Acts 6:9–10)

Much like Jesus, Stephen faced zealous opposition from members of the Synagogue. The consequences of such opposition included increased scrutiny, which eventually led to violence. The challenge Stephen presented to his opposers was that they could neither support their argument nor refute his argument. They were confounded but not convinced.It was evident that the wisdom and the Spirit by which Stephen spoke was the manifestation of the promise Jesus made in Luke 21:15. There is no human argument or logic that can dispute with the Spirit of God

Message Point 3: The Truth Shines Bright (Acts 6:11–7:2a)

It would have been a normal, human reaction for Stephen to be scared or shaken after being put in such a position. Some people struggle with public speaking even when there is no malicious intent on the part of the listeners. But Stephen's face shone as an external sign of his internal revelation and confidence. His response and countenance shone brightly in the face of opposition. Even their schemes could not detract from the facts that Stephen was saying with his words and displaying with his body.

THAT'LL PREACH

The 2019 film, Just Mercy, details the story of Walter McMillian, a Black man sentenced to death for the murder of a white woman that he did not commit, and Bryan Stevenson, the lawyer who fought his case. McMillian was imprisoned because of a false testimony, much like Stephen in today's text. The courts could not refute the evidence that showed McMillian was innocent. As Walter was persecuted and punished because of his identity, so Stephen was targeted for his faith. Even though Stephen's case had a different outcome, he still stood up for what he believed.

CONCLUSION

The assault on the believer and the Church comes in many different ways. When adversaries fail to derail the ministry of God, they resort to other means of disputing. When the Gospel prevails in the Church, it is prosecuted in the courts; when it prevails in the courts, it is prosecuted in the media. Evil forces become more enraged when their presence, influence, and motives are exposed for what they are. Stephen proved his adversary to be wrong, for which he was criminally charged and executed. Though faithfully proving his case, Stephen became an enemy of the government and the people. What courage does it take for a believer today to witness in a society of counterfeit believers and religious zealots? What courage does it take for a believer to oppose spiritual imposters who pervert and distort the Word of God to exploit God's people? Stephen's undaunted courage sets an example of what countenance Christians can have in the face of imminent danger. Like Stephen, believers today can be transformed and armed with undisturbed serenity, free from fear for ourselves and free from anger towards persecutors.

NOTES

Stephen's Martyrdom

By Elder George Akins, Jr.

Lesson Theme	Unit Theme	Scripture
Stephen's Martyrdom	A Living Faith	Acts 7:51–8:1a

INTRODUCTION

When holy leaders confront traditional religious and cultural ideas, their words may incite anger and violence. Stephen's criticism of the religious establishment and his exaltation of Christ enraged the religious leaders of his day. Stephen's stoning similarly repeats the terms and conditions surrounding the crucifixion of Jesus. His belief caused his death, seemingly at the hands of an angry mob. This text reveals how the sacrifice of one can produce good for many.

MESSAGE POINTS

Message Point 1: From Past to Present (Acts 7:51–53)

Stephen's speech calls out an ancestral track record of willful and stubborn resistance. By using words and phrases like "Hard heart, obstinate, and contumacious" reveals the unyielding character of Biblical Israel (Exodus 32:9; 33:3, 5; 34:9; Deuteronomy 9:6, 13; 31:27; Ezekiel 2:4, 2) This memory includes the various methods and times God used to reach, reclaim, and reform His people. But unfortunately they remained uncircumcised in heart and ears; not devoted or given to God. Even after all of this history, the persecution of Stephen points to a people resolved not to comply with God either by Law of the Old Testament or by the Gospel of the New Testament

Message Point 2: Prayer (Acts 7:55, 56, 59, 60)

Stephen's prayers in his final moments indicate a close relationship with God. He received courage and comfort in the midst of persecution and used the opportunity to express his awe at the glory of God and the Son of Man. Stephen also offers a prayer of supplication for God to receive his spirit. He also asks for forgiveness for thse who are harming him. This shows how the light of heaven can converge with and overcome the darkness of hell. While the strength of corruption decomposes humanity, the strength of Spirit composes humanity.

Message Point 3: Paul Also Present (Acts 8:1a)

The end of Stephen's life and witness also acts as a foreshadowing of a new beginning. At this point, Paul is still Saul. Because of his religious zeal, he approved of what had been done to Stephen. This shows that witness may not come to fruition instantly, yet we should continue to offer our best testimony no matter the situation. You never know who is listening or watching. Stephen's life and testimony was a seed planted in the dark that eventually bloomed in the life and work of Paul.

THAT'LL PREACH

While social media can be a space for information sharing, entertainment, and connection, it can also be a hostile place for truth-tellers. Many activists have used online spaces such as Twitter to keep people informed and safe. But they often face the vitriol of internet "trolls." From being called slurs to doxing, revealing personal information such as a person's address or phone number, truth-tellers face many forms of violence. And just like in today's text, there are those who actively participate in this violence as well as those who sit on the sidelines without interfering. As believers standing up for our faith, we have to decide what kind of role we will play.

CONCLUSION

Enmity toward God is heart–cutting, while faith and love are heart–healing. Those who reject God and oppose God's power and presence are really tormentors to themselves. Their angry behavior toward the Church and believers today serves as an expression of anger perhaps because of the lack of ability to reason. Hence, when reasoning fails, people sometimes resort to emotional extremes. The witness of believers today is similar to that of Stephen's in a profoundly fundamental way. Believers' composure and comfort of soul, thrust into a world of terrifying hatred, still permits the Church to enjoy the fellowship of Christ amid the confusion and decadence of a rejecting world. As the world continually attempts to put Christ to death, believers continually attempt to endure and survive persecution through the power of the Holy Spirit.

NOTES

Simon Wants to Buy Power

By Elder George Akins, Jr.

Lesson Theme	Unit Theme	Scripture
Simon Wants to Buy Power	A Living Faith	Acts 8:9–24

INTRODUCTION

Philip preached the things concerning the Kingdom of God, it's constitution, and the liberties and privileges of it, including the power of healing and the power of the Holy Spirit. He preached it in its commanding power and influence and the people believed him. Up to that time, Simon the magician had enjoyed the respect and reputation of being God's man of power, growing accustomed to the accolades bestowed upon him. Upon becoming a believer, he desired to have the same power he had witnessed at the hands of Philip and the apostles. He was so desperate to have it that he offered to buy it. His proposition was met with the sharp rebuke of Peter and a warning. The Holy Spirit, Peter plainly laid out, is God's gift; one that can neither be bought nor sold for the perverted purposes that Simon intended.

MESSAGE POINTS

Message Point 1: Pride, Ambition, and an Affectation of Grandeur (Acts 8:9–11)

Simon had become accustomed to a certain lifestyle where he was recognized as someone powerful so he had a puffed up sense of pride. He was a man of great ambition and he had a propensity for grandeur. But the power he possessed was distinct from what the Apostles displayed. Magic is no comparison to the signs and wonders made possible by the power of the Spirit.

Message Point 2: Converted or Contrived (Acts 8:13–18)

Here we see Simon's conversion and close attention to the activity of the Apostles. Philip's activity shows the purpose of miracles as an evangelism tool and the purpose of baptism as an initiation to the community. There is also an apparent duty to fellowship with newly converted. Jerusalem acts as a point of coordination for the growing Church. Besides administrative assistance, this emerging community was in need of something more urgent: the power of the Holy Spirit. This manifested in the laying of hands, showing that there is something special about physical presence.

Message Point 3: Converted But Still in Bondage (Acts 8:20–24)

While Simon had believed enough to be baptized, he had not understood fully the power of the Spirit. This transformation had yet to take place. The secrets of the heart as seen by God were revealed in his attempt to buy this power that is freely given. The ambition that had previously characterized his life and work indicated a Contingent Discipleship: seeking primarily the benefit of bread and miracles. They say old habits die hard, but we see Simon's conviction in his immediate request for prayer. Change takes time, especially when one has made gain their whole life.

THAT'LL PREACH

There are many "get rich quick" and pyramid schemes that entrap people today. Those who promote these products and services prey on the vulnerabilities of those in financial need. Some people are desperate enough to risk their life savings for the possibilities of getting rich. But these schemes usually end up hurting people not only financially, but also mentally and physically. Perhaps Simon thought power of the Holy Spirit would be one way for him to make more money than his sorcery scheme, but the apostles' rebuke showed him how powerful this gift truly is, not a scheme but the very Spirit of God.

CONCLUSION

The laying of hands is anciently used in blessing by those who had authority to do so. It was the Apostle Peter who discerned that Simon's wicked proposal was an espousal of his heart. Simon apparently believed that the gift of the Holy Spirit was commensurate to an exalted piece of sorcery, thus making him equal to Peter and John and himself capable of conferring the same gift. Peter's discernment confronts Simon's motive not to participate in the spread of the Gospel but merely to regain a place of prominence and prestige lost upon the arrival of Philip. Simon was more interested in honor for himself than the good of others. His aim was the reward of divination. He offered money in exchange for the money he hoped to gain by it. His thinking overvalued the wealth of the world while undervaluing the wealth of God.

We are as our hearts are. We speak and act out of the abundance of the heart. If our hearts are correct toward God, the work of God, and the people of God, then we are open to be judged by them. Our hearts are open to the sight of God, who cannot be deceived. We can accept the call to repentance of the Apostle Peter and the encouragement to pray that the deeds of our heart may be forgiven.

NOTES

Faith that Guides

By Elder George Akins, Jr.

Lesson Theme	Unit Theme	Scripture
Philip and the Ethiopian Eunuch	A Living Faith	Acts 8:26–38

INTRODUCTION

Acting under divine instructions of a messenger angel, Philip is directed to a road where he meets the Ethiopian secretary of treasury. Although it may not be widely heard of today, ministers and believers are subject to the deployment of God's action plan to achieve God's strategic objectives. Philip may never have considered traveling such a minor road compared to major routes he could have chosen. Yet he goes to a deserted, wilderness path leading into the desert of Judah southward to Ethiopia. Sometimes God opens doors of opportunity to minister in unlikely places to unlikely people. Let's examine the context of Philip's encounter with the Ethiopian and determine how Philip assumed full advantage of the opportunity.

MESSAGE POINTS

Message Point 1: A Matter of Perspective: Boundary or Opportunity (Acts 8:26–28)

Without the intervention of the angel of the Lord, this scene could have been characterized by cultural biases. The enuch may have been stigmatized by reputation and race. Upon hearing his reading, Philip recognizes the Ethiopian's power and dignity. This leads to an invitation for fellowship

Message Point 2: A New Learning Experience (Acts 8:29–35)

Though it was not in Philip's original route or plan, he engages in a non-traditional learning experience. The chariot acts as the synagogue. The teacher-learner and learner-teacher are seated side-by-side, not one above the other. The eunuch is able to voice his questions without reproach. Philip is attentive to the concerns of the student. Instead of acting as "sage on the stage," Philip's teaching style can be characterized as a "guide on the side."

Message Point 3: Spontaneous Baptism (Acts 8:36–38)

It would stand to reason that a non-traditional baptism experience would follow this non-traditional learning experience. The eunuch's request demonstrates a sense of urgency motivated by what he has just learned about the good news of Jesus. Philip continues to adapt to this new learning context and in doing so fulfills the prediction of Acts 1:8. This event is also significant in that it broke social and ritual barriers.

THAT'LL PREACH

A man was on his way to an important interview for his dream job. If he could land it, it would give him and his family the financial boost they needed to finally own their own home. As he was driving down the busy main road, he noticed a car on the shoulder with its hazard lights blinking. Even though he was in a rush, he knew what it was like to be stuck on the side of the road waiting hours for AAA. He pulled over and was able to help the driver fix the issue with the car. After finishing, he barely made it in time for his interview, entering the building at the same time as the head of the HR department, who happened to be his interviewer and the driver he had just helped! You never know what a blessing it can be to go a little off–course.

CONCLUSION

The business of Gospel ministers is to preach Jesus, and this is the preaching that is likely to do good and win souls. It is probable that the Ethiopian had heard of the doctrine of Christ while he was in Jerusalem. It may not have been new to him. It was still the working of the Holy Spirit that enabled Philip to gain a new convert along a less traveled path leading into the desert. God's provisions always seem to accompany opportunities. The sight of water triggered the idea in the mind of the Ethiopians that baptism was properly in order. He made no delay in demonstrating his dedication and devotion to God. Like the Ethiopian, the present time is the best time for us to obey the commandments of God.

NOTES

Paul Before King Agrippa

By Dr. James Rawdon

Lesson Theme	Unit Theme	Scripture
Paul before King Agrippa	A Living Faith	Acts 26:19–32

INTRODUCTION

A living faith leads to a vibrant witness. Paul's commitment to Christ and the Gospel led him to a great opportunity to proclaim the Kingship of Christ to top government officials.

MESSAGE POINTS

Message Point 1: Paul's Situation (Acts 25:13–15, 25–27)

Acts 25 details how and why Festus, the new governor of Palestine (Acts 24:27–25:1:6), brought Paul's situation, being imprisoned in Caesarea for two years (Acts 24:27a), to the attention of Agrippa, regional overseer of a small region in Palestine but also of the Temple. But instead of focusing on his own freedom, Paul uses this as an opportunity to talk about what Jesus had done in his life and the mission he was called to.

Message Point 2: Paul's Defense (Acts 26:1–18)

The first step in Paul's defense was to establish rapport with his listeners. He proceeds with an identification with orthodox Judaism and his defense of it (Acts 26:4–12; 1 Kings 17:17–22; 2 Kings 4:32–35, 13:20–21).He also describes his encounter with Jesus on the way to Damascus and Jesus' commission.

Message Point 3: Paul's Testimony (Acts 26:19–23)

Paul continues his testimony with an acceptance of the reality of the heavenly vision. Paul positively respons to Jesus' commission and describes the extent of his obedience. The content of Paul's message included repentance, turning away from sin, and turning to God and detailed a lifestyle worthy of repentance. There was criminal violence in response to Paul's testimony. Kill literally means lay hands on, which indicates physical attack. Paul had experienced this before (Acts 14:19). Paul's witness continues with Jesus' fulfillment of Jewish expectations from Moses (Deuteronomy 18:15–18) to the prophets (Isaiah 53:4–9; Zechariah 12:10).

Message Point 4: Responding to Rejection and Disbelief (Acts 26:24–32)

Festus' responds with a loud rejection. There was the common reaction of laughter, scorn, and questioning.Paul shows that we should always have a ready response (1 Peter 3:14) and deliver it "in a gentle and respectful way" (1 Peter 3:15a). Paul also responded to their avoidance—including Agrippa. Paul demonstrates how to use present understanding as a starting point for witnessing. He was also intentional in his use of everyday language, not religious clichés (Colossians 4:6). He also assumed spiritual interest: "I know thou believest." (Acts 26:27). He also responded to their delay by testifying to assurance of the personal benefit of your faith (Acts 26:29), attesting to the benefit in spite of personal limitations: "except these bonds". He showed that God works through faithful and consistent witness (Philippians 1:27). Faithful witness furthers consideration of the

Gospel. Paul's eloquent defense and testimony show how God's Holy Spirit brings consideration and conviction of truth (John 16:7–11).

THAT'LL PREACH

In the 2015 Rocky spin-off film, *Creed*, Adonis Creed trains with Rocky Balboa to become a boxing champion. At the end of the film, Adonis loses the final fight by a split decision. But in the process, he proved himself to be a worthy opponent by being the first fighter to knock Conlan down. He earns the respect of the crowd and of Rocky himself. In a similar way, although Paul did not "win" before Agrippa, he put up a powerful fight for his faith and left a lasting impression on all who listened to his witness.

CONCLUSION

Paul didn't have "success" in evangelizing Agrippa and Festus, but his example is a true glimpse of a faithful life.

NOTES

Paul Sails to Rome

By Dr. James Rawdon

Lesson Theme	Unit Theme	Scripture
Paul Sails for Rome	A Living Faith	Acts 27:1–2, 33–44

INTRODUCTION

How do you respond in times of crisis? Do you set your witness aside, or seize the opportunity to proclaim the truth and power of the Gospel?

MESSAGE POINTS

Message Point 1: From Jail on Land to Jail at Sea (Acts 27:1–2)

According to Acts 24:27, Paul had been in prison on land for two years under the rule of Felix. He was then transferred under the supervision of a centurion named Julius, along with Aristarchus, a Christian convert, Paul's companion (Acts 19:29; Philemon 24) and fellow prisoner (Colossians 4:10). The dangerous winter voyage had a slow, uncertain beginning.

Message Point 2: From Concern to Confusion to Crisis (Acts 27:20, 27, 29–34)

Despite the measures taken by the crew, their situation began to seem hopeless. Paul warns against the danger of not eating. Stress and anxiety tend to take a toll on the whole body, especially affecting the digestive system. Those aboard the ship also had to consider how to ration what food they did have but were unsure how long they would be lost at sea. Paul then encourages self preservation and reassures them of God's promises.

Message Point 3: From Acute Fear to Active Faith (Acts 27:35–38)

In the midst of the crisis, Paul takes the opportunity to offer a public prayer, thus showing the importance of active faith. Paul made his faith visible in preparing for survival. Our action confirms the reality of our faith (James 2:14–18). This embodied, lived out faith has the potential for encouraging others. Faith's effect helps clarify thinking about further action when stuck between a rock and a hard place.

Message Point 4: The Practical Results of Faith for the Future (Acts 27:39–41)

Like Paul and all those aboard that ship, we need a living faith. A living faith for facing the unknown, for planning to act, and for courage to cope with the unexpected. Their plan was ruined by a reef they could not see. Sometimes situations we did not anticipate appear in our lives and drive us off course. Then we, like the crew, must make do with what we have around us in order to survive.

Message Point 5: The Predictable and Unpredictable Responses to Faith's Example (Acts 27:42–44)
The plan to kill the prisoners could be considered the predictable response of sinful self-interest , but it also reveals the harsh requirements of Roman law for allowing escape, confirming the soldier's understandable motivation to fear punishment. And yet Julius offers an unpredictable response to Paul's prophecy. He wished to save one but ended up facilitating the fulfillment of Paul's prophecy: all 276 on board survive. Allies can be found in the most unlikely places.

THAT'LL PREACH

From 1914-1917, Ernest Shackleton embarked on an expedition in Antarctica with a crew of 22 men. His ship, the Endurance, became trapped in ice. While Shackleton and the crew made camp on the ice, the abandoned ship eventually disappeared underwater. Stuck on a remote island, they still resolved to get help. Shackleton and five other men set out in a 20–foot lifeboat for the island of South Georgia with the intent of sending rescue back for the remaining men. Miraculously, after an incredibly perilous journey that included riding out hurricane-force winds and trekking 32 miles across dangerous terrain, they did exactly that. After surviving for four and a half months, the entire crew was rescued. Surviving a shipwreck is no small feat, especially with over 200 people on board. Paul also demonstrated great leadership and faith in the face of crisis.

CONCLUSION

God honored Paul and revealed His truth and power in this shipwreck. What is your witness when shipwreck comes your way?

NOTES

Paul Ministers in Malta

Dr. James Rawdon

Lesson Theme	Unit Theme	Scripture
Paul Ministers in Malta	A Living Faith	Acts 28:1–10

INTRODUCTION

Paul sought to honor God everywhere he went. Today, we see how Paul continued to be a living witness to the Gospel in a new situation and new place.

MESSAGE POINTS

Message Point 1: Paul's Prophecy is Fulfilled (Acts 27:24–26).
Paul and company find themselves on the island of Melita, now called Malta, which was more than 1,200 miles from Caesarea where they embarked and more than 400 miles from Rome, their destination. When the text calls the people of Malta "barbarous" it did not mean that the islanders were heartless pagans but simply that they did not speak Greek. The language barrier did not prove to be a hospitality barrier. All 276 survivors were wet but cared for, requiring not one, but many fires in the rainy and cold weather. Storm wind had wrecked the ship and worsened the cold's effect. Building fires in windy rain demanded the utmost effort, a form of radical hospitality.

Message Point 2: Paul's Part in a Common Confusion Over the Causes of Good or Bad (Acts 28:3–6)
Paul's run-in with a viper caused confusion over why bad happens to good people. Working after surviving a shipwreck showed Paul's initiative but the islanders had assumed bad things like a snake bite only happened to bad people, such as murderers . Sometimes there is similar confusion over the cause of good experiences. But Paul's reaction of shaking the snake off and continuing to work showed faith and the assurance of God's care. The islanders mistakenly assumed surviving a poisonous snake's bite could only happen to a divine being, show that Christian witness requires overcoming many misconceptions.

Message Point 3: Paul's Acceptance of Needed Help Used to Show God's Power and Love (Acts 28:7–8)
People without God are not without God-given compassion (1 Kings 8:50). Publius' kindness to Paul and others allowed Paul to see a need for ministry and witness. Ministry meant Paul encountered unpleasant needs: "fever and ... a bloody flux." Ministry meant Paul confronted his own human susceptibility to disease: " Paul entered in" Ministry meant Paul trusted God's power to meet the man's problem: "and prayed." Ministry meant Paul's willingness to involve himself in the man's situation: "and laid his hands on him." Ministry meant God worked a miraculous result through Paul's initiative, faith, and willingness to involve himself in the man's problem.

Message Point 4: Revealed larger needs and opened more opportunities for ministry and witness (Acts 28:9–10).

Paul's ministry to Publius' father revealed a greater scope of needs. A greater understanding of human needs required a greater faith and a greater willingness to become involved with needy persons by Paul and fellow Christians. Paul's willingness to respond to human neediness created a positive attitude toward those committed to the Gospel of Jesus Christ and a willingness to share in it.

THAT'LL PREACH

Snake bites are a serious matter. Take one hiker's experience with a rattlesnake for example: "After the bite, my small (5'4", 100 pounds) body immediately started reacting to the toxins coursing through it. My system was pumped full of adrenaline, so I wasn't initially in pain, but I was frantic with fear. The near-lethal doses of venom worked quickly, beginning to incapacitate me within minutes...Bruises and blisters start forming around the bite site within a half hour, the venom's digestive action starts melting tissue near the wound within six hours, and a victim might suffer aches and nausea for days." No wonder the people of Malta were so shocked that Paul was able to shake the snake off and live to tell the tale.

Source: Kristy Holland, "Out Alive: Survive a Rattlesnake Bite," Backpacker Magazine, May 30, 2012, https://www.backpacker.com/survival/out-alive-survive-a-rattlesnake-bite/.

CONCLUSION

Do you look for opportunities to share the truth of the Gospel in different situations and places? God will be with us and honor us as we share the Good News with others through our words and deeds.

NOTES

Paul Evangelizes in Rome

By Dr. Vincent Bacote

Lesson Theme	Unit Theme	Scripture
Paul Evangelizes in Rome	A Living Faith	Acts 28:23–31

INTRODUCTION

Paul's life reveals a zeal for spreading the hope of the Gospel. His example offers us an inspiring challenge to know and communicate God's truth.

MESSAGE POINTS

Message Point 1: Telling the Story All Day Long (v. 23)
Paul preached to a large Jewish crowd in his dwelling from morning to night, even while under house arrest. Paul revealed how Jesus fulfills the message of the law and prophets. Paul sought to persuade the crowd of the Gospel truth. This is what he was imprisoned for, but remained passionate about. Even when the authorities tried to stop him, the people came flocking to him. When there is a call on one's life, God will always make a way.

Message Point 2: Responding to the Mixed Reaction (v. 24–28)
The Gospel is a divisive message: Some will believe, and some will resist. This has been and continues to be the reaction. Isaiah's prophecy is fulfilled in the resistance of those who won't believe. The Gospel authoris also used this passage from Isaiah to talk about Israel's rejectino of of the good news. Paul's larger mission: spreading the Gospel to all people. Instead of getting upset or hung up on who was not listening, Paul rejoiced in those who would. This is not a final rejection of the Jewish people, but a reflection of the social reality of the time in which Paul is preaching. Even if the reaction is mixed, the seed is still being planted.

Message Point 3: Proclaiming the Good News in Rome (v. 30–31)
Paul is an example of a bi-vocational preacher. He lived in his own hired dwelling and before his arrest, he worked as a tentmaker to support himself and his ministry (Acts 181–4). Paul also had an "open door policy" that showed that all inquirers are welcome, not just the ones who would agree with him or support him. Paul's apostolic vigor demonstrates how to preach with boldness. Paul's ministry under house arrest continued for two years, showing just how committed he was to sharing the Gospel.

THAT'LL PREACH

Like Paul, Martin Luther King, Jr. continued to preach and write letters to key communities while in prison. In his 1963 "Letter from a Birmingham Jail," he urges white Christians to stand with their African American siblings in the face of economic and racial injustice. Consider his words, "I am in Birmingham because injustice is here. We are like the eighth-century prophets Amos, Hosea, Jonah, and Micah, who left their little villages and carried their "thus saith the Lord" far beyond their hometowns. We are like the Apostle Paul, who left his little village of Tarsus and carried the words of Jesus Christ to almost every village and city in the Greek and Roman world. Moreover, I am aware of how all cities and states are connected to one another. I cannot sit in Atlanta watching what is happening in Birmingham. Injustice anywhere is a threat to justice everywhere."

CONCLUSION

Paul preached to everyone even while he was under house arrest. How do we proclaim our faith when we are free? How do we provide a witness when we are under duress? Paul knew God was with him. God is with us as well. Let's be living witnesses!

NOTES

Spiritual Blessings in Jesus Christ

By Matthew C. Jones

Lesson Theme	Unit Theme	Scripture
Spiritual Blessings in Jesus Christ	Jesus Is Lord	Ephesians 1:3–14

INTRODUCTION

Setting and Context of Ephesians

The letter to the church in Ephesus was drafted by Apostle Paul who is imprisoned in Rome and is dated A.D. 60–61. It was delivered by Tychicus, "who is carrying this letter" (6:21–22).

Supremacy of Christ in Ephesians

Jesus is supreme in salvation and over all creation, especially the powers of darkness. Jesus is supreme in sanctification, bringing all people together as one army in spiritual battle. Jesus is supreme in society, unifying families, races, and classes as a single body.

Starting the Correspondence of Ephesians

The churches of Asia Minor are facing division, darkness, and doubts. Paul reaffirms his charge "by the will of God" (Ephesians 1:1). He begins the letter by invoking the comfort of the Almighty God (Ephesians 1:2).

MESSAGE POINTS

The Blessings of the Triune God in the Gospel (Ephesians 1:3–14)

Message Point 1: The Father Who Elects (1:3–6)

This section is based on a traditional Jewish prayer that focuses on God's actions on behalf of Israel. The Father is praised for giving spiritual blessings and the greatest blessing of all, Jesus Christ. (v. 3) The predestination of the Father emphasizes Jesus as the mediator of these divine blessings (v. 4). To be chosen echoes back to the Old Testament identification of Israel as God's people. It gives the Father pleasure to adopt us into His family. Adoption signifies both intimacy as well as the rights and responsibilities of being God's children. (v. 5).

Message Point 2: The Son Who Emancipates (vv. 7–12)

Jesus redeems us from sin (vv. 7–8). This redemption is akin to being rescued, released, or ransomed from slavery. The debt we owed was paid with Jesus' blood on the Cross. Jesus reveals the mystery of salvation (v. 9). Here there is unification of the Church and the cosmos, what was once out of reach or unintelliglbe has become accessible thanks to Jesus. Jesus reigns as sovereign (vv. 10–12). Paul continues to use the language of inheritance and adoption. He also acknowledges the early Jewish followers of the Christian movement.

Message Point 3: The Holy Spirit Who Ensures (vv. 13–14)
The Gospel brings salvation (v. 13). One must hear and also believe. This saving truth is available for both Jews and Gentiles. The seal of the promised Holy Spirit indicates ownership and protection. In Galatians 3, Paul traces the promise of the Holy Spirit all the way back to Abraham (Gal. 3:14, 22). The pledge or guarantee of the Spirit can be seen as a first installment (v. 14a) of this long-awaited promise.

THAT'LL PREACH

This passage ends with the promise of an inheritance. Sometimes issues of inheritance cause stress and strife within families. How wonderful to have a guaranteed inheritance with the rest of our siblings in the faith. There is enough to go around! This promised inheritance also brings joy compared to other types of inheritance. People usually receive an inheritance when a loved one passes away. Instead, we have an inheritance from the One who died but rose again and now lives forever. More precious than money, a house, land, or jewels, this is the hope we have in Jesus Christ!

CONCLUSION

KNOW: God blesses believers with all spiritual benefits in heavenly places in Christ by the power of the Gospel.

- The Gospel overwhelms the darkness.
- The Gospel heals division.
- The Gospel brings deliverance.

FEEL: God blesses believers with adoption into His family as children by the work of Christ, the Son of God.

- We are atoned by Christ.
- We are adopted by the Father.
- We are authenticated by the Spirit.

DO: God blesses believers with assurance by the seal of the Holy Spirit sent from Christ.

- Assurance from "every spiritual blessing" (v. 3)
- Assurance from the election of God (v. 5, 11)
- Assurance from the endorsement of the Spirit (vv. 13–14)

NOTES

One in Jesus Christ

By Matthew C. Jones

Lesson Theme	Unit Theme	Scripture
One in Jesus Christ	Jesus Is Lord	Ephesians 2:11–22

INTRODUCTION

The Salvation We Don't Deserve that Comes by Grace (Ephesians 2:1–10)

Paul explains how we were once dead in sin (vv. 1–4) but have now come alive in the Son (vv. 5–7) by grace from the Savior (vv. 8–10). This applies to everyone, Jews and Gentiles alike. What do we do now that we have received this amazing grace? How are we to treat one another, even those who are different from us?

MESSAGE POINTS

Corporate Reconciliation and Oneness in Christ (Ephesians 2:11–22)

Message Point 1: The Gentiles Apart from God's Covenant (Ephesians 2:11–12)

God is a covenant maker to His people. God entered into a covenant with Israel through His patriarchs and prophets. But the Gentiles were ejected by the circumcised (v. 11) and excluded from citizenship in Israel (v. 12a), leaving them empty of hope and God (v. 12b). That is, until God's covenant extends to us in His promised Son.

Message Point 2: The Gentiles Accepted in God's New Covenant (Ephesians 2:13–14)

We have been given hope through the Gospel. We have no hindrances in the Gospel to being a united body. We have a new head, Jesus Christ, who is in charge of the Church. This is what it means to be "Brought near through the blood of Christ" (v. 13). Because Jesus "is our peace" (v. 14), barriers are removed (v. 14).

Message Point 3: The Gentiles are One Body (Ephesians 2:15–22)

The Church should have a diversity of people and unity in God's will. The Church should grieve division over nonessentials and bring unity in Christ.The Church should defend the oppressed and invite all people into the promises of God. Death to the flesh brings "one new man out of the two" (v. 15). Divisive hostility has ended and peace has come (vv. 16–17). Dwelling within Gentiles and Jews, God has a new temple (vv. 18–22).

THAT'LL PREACH

This passage discusses people of different cultures coming together, united by their faith in Christ. This simultaneous diversity and unity has always been part of God's plan for God's people. Remember at the Tower of Babel (Genesis 11:1–9), the people were given different languages, the start of the linguistic diversity we see in our world today. Such diversity was again reflected when the Holy Spirit descended on the Early Church (Acts 2). Remember the Gentile women included in Jesus' genealogy (Matthew 1:2–16), those who might have expected to be excluded because of their gender and national origin but played integral roles in story of our Savior. God has consistently shown us that the Body of Christ is diverse and purposely so.

CONCLUSION

KNOW: Salvation reveals God's plan of redeeming the nations through Israel by the work of Christ in fulfilling the law of Moses and bringing the New Covenant through His atoning life, death, and resurrection.

FEEL: Salvation reconciles unworthy sinners to God and brings them into a reconciled community that is the very family of God through the gracious work of the Son.

DO: Salvation releases joy in us as we are freed from hatred, discrimination, ethnocentrism, and an oppressive society. Christ's power breaks down all dividing walls and brings His people together as one diverse family to display the work of the one true and living God.

NOTES

Unity in the Body of Christ

By Matthew C. Jones

Lesson Theme	Unit Theme	Scripture
Unity in the Body of Christ	Jesus Is Lord	Ephesians 4:1–16

INTRODUCTION

- The providence of God who is sovereign (Ephesians 1)
- The provision of God who saves (Ephesians 2:1–10)
- The people of God who serve in unity (Ephesians 2:11–3:21)

MESSAGE POINTS

The People of Christ in Community (Ephesians 4:1–16)

Message Point 1: The Walk of the One Body of Christ (Ephesians 4:1–6)

"Live a life worthy of the calling you have received" even if you are imprisoned in body, your spirit is free. This requires patient love for God's people and peaceful unity in God. Love the Church through humility, peacefulness, and gentleness. Let the truth be known to preserve the unity of the Spirit.We have one faith, so there is pure doctrine. We have one Father, God, so there is paternal affection. We have one foundation, so there is pastoral calling.

Message Point 2: The Work of the Historic Christ (Ephesians 4:7–10)

The grace of Christ is indicated as a gift from Him. Psalm 68:18 is used here to describe how Christ ascended and gifted His Church for ministry. The glory of Christ is evident in His ascension and reminds us that He is the head of all things. He is the perfect role model. While we can never achieve His level of divinty, we can aspire to live lives that honor His work as a teacher, prophet, evangelist, friend, and even political radical.

Message Point 3: The Witness of the Church of Christ (Ephesians 4:11–16)

Leaders acknowledge their duty to equip the Church for "the work of service" (v. 12). Believers all play a role in "the growth of the body" (v. 16). The offices named are foundational leaders for building the church but there are other roles that are just as important. Those who serve food, shovel snow, and express other forms of radical hospitality are also included in the building up and the witness of the Church. Demonstrating faithful unity indicates maturity in Christ (vv. 13–14). No longer vulnerable infants who cannot do much for themselves, from Christ, the head, we grow (vv. 15–16).

THAT'LL PREACH

A lot of people experience "growing pains" as children. They feel an ache or soreness in their legs, especially at night. While this might be caused by overuse throughout the day, it is still a sign of the body's growth and development. Children grow into adolescents and experience hormonal changes. Eventually these adolescents become adults with new responsibilities and expectations. In each phase of development, the body may experience pain. But that pain could be a sign of development for the better. The Body of Christ may experience pain but if we are united, we can endure and grow into who God has called us to be.

CONCLUSION

KNOW: There is deep unity in the body of Christ that God has sovereignly provided for us to experience and share.

FEEL: There is doctrinal truth that binds the Church, granting a unity in the faith and knowledge of God that protects us from spiritual errors and imposters.

DO: There is delightful work for us to carry out by the baptizing Spirit who unites, gifts, and matures us in the fullness of Christ.

NOTES

Reassurance for God's People

By Rev. Robert J. Morgan

Lesson Theme	Unit Theme	Scripture
According to the Promise	Jesus Is Lord	Luke 1:39–54

INTRODUCTION

You wouldn't think it by taking a shopping trip to our affluent malls, but Christmas began as a very humble event, an event that exhibited the greatest humility the world has ever seen—the God of glory being laid in a cattle trough. We see:

MESSAGE POINTS

Message Point 1: Humility Exhibited in Mary's Situation (Luke 1:39)
Everything about Mary was humble— her hometown, her poverty, her hardships, her displacement in Bethlehem, her entire setting (2:1–4).

Message Point 2: Humility Expressed in Mary's Song (1:46–54)
In her Magnificat, she spoke of how God resists the proud but exalts the lowly.

Message Point 3: Humility Exemplified in Mary's Son (v. 54)
Jesus came, "Out of the Ivory Palaces, into a world of woe" (see Psalm 45).

THAT'LL PREACH

SPOILER ALERT: In the story "A Christmas Carol" by Charles Dickens the main character Ebenezer Scrooge valued money over everything else. He was a wealthy man, who saw others in need all around him but did not have the heart to help. After being warned several times by the ghost of his deceased business partner and the Ghosts of Christmas Past, Present, and Future, Scrooge came to the realization that it is not money or positions that bring joy but love. Love inspires community, love inspires generosity, and love inspires sacrifice. This Christmas, before we run out to the stores or begin our online shopping, let's take a moment to remember God's love for us and the sacrifice Jesus made so that we could have a direct relationship with God.

CONCLUSION

We take pride in birth and rank, but Jesus was a carpenter's son. We take pride in possessions, but He had nowhere to lay His head. Is there any way in which we can observe Christmas with the personal humility that reflects our Saviour? God exalts the proud, but gives grace to the humble.

NOTES

Christ's Love for the Church

By Matthew C. Jones

Lesson Theme	Unit Theme	Scripture
Christ's Love for the Church	Jesus Is Lord	Ephesians 5:21–6:4

INTRODUCTION

- God created humanity in His image for family and loving relationships.
- Sin corrupted humanity and the family, bringing guilt and broken relationships into the world.
- The Son came into humanity as a man in a family to redeem sinners into the family of God.

MESSAGE POINTS

Family Matters (Ephesians 5)

Message Point 1: The Love of a Wife Reflects the Love of the Church for Christ (5:22–24).

- Husbands and wives should submit to one another as a witness of Christ's love
- Wives should submit to their husband meaning they respect their position and give deference to their leadership as they are led by Christ.
- Husbands serve in leadership for their homes. It is a matter of position not nature and not an invitation to abuse or domination.

Message Point 2: The Love of a Husband Reflecting the Passion of the Christ (5:25–33)

- Husbands should "die daily" for their wives.
- Husbands should share and live out the Word of Christ, cleansing their wives in the Scripture.

Message Point 3: The Love of a Parent Reflects the Instruction of Christ (6:1–4).

- Parents should direct their children as honorable examples worthy of obedience.
- Parents should discipline and instruct their children.

THAT'LL PREACH

Understanding your love language as well as the love language of those you are in relationship with can have great benefits. The Five Love Languages, created by Gary Chapman, are as follows: Acts of Service, Words of Affirmation, Quality Time, Physical Touch, and Gifts. When special occasions come around, we stress about finding the perfect gift for our loved one. But in reality they might appreciate a hand-written letter or being able to spend time with you. Sometimes we misunderstand each other, not because we lack love, but because we have not communicated in the appropriate love language. Take the time to get to know yourself and your loved ones in a new way.

CONCLUSION

KNOW: Christ loved the Church with all of His being. He died for her and defeated the power of death, satisfying the penalty of our sin, bringing believers into relationship with God and each other as family members.

FEEL: Christ lived in sacrifice to show His love for the Church with the intimacy of marriage and the care of a perfect husband, sacrificing and serving.

DO: Christ leads as our example, so we confront the demands of our world that move us away from home to live in acceptance of our responsibility to love our families as Christ demonstrated His love for the Church.

NOTES

Proclaiming Christ

By Dr. Brian Bantum

Lesson Theme	Unit Theme	Scripture
Proclaiming Christ	Jesus is Lord	Philippians 1:15–26

INTRODUCTION

It is true that some preach Christ out of envy and rivalry, but others out of goodwill. But what does it matter (v. 1:15–17)? There is always the possibility that Christ's work can become an idol. In our zeal, passion, and hope, Christ's work becomes bound within our vision of the Good News. Paul's exhortation reminds us that it is the power of Christ's life and work that makes the news good. Because of this unalterable power of Christ's life, the power of the preached Word cannot be sullied by the perfection or imperfection of our words. And yet, what does it matter? Surely, our words matter. Surely the shape of our lives together matter. Does the power of Christ's life and the simple fact that Christ is preached regardless of the life of the one who speaks, not count for something?

MESSAGE POINTS

Message Point 1: Preaching Christ—But what does it matter?

The important thing is that in every way, whether from false motives or true, Christ is preached. And because of this I rejoice (v. 18). Paul leads us into the dangerous truth of preaching the Gospel, of preaching Christ crucified: Preaching Christ is not a means to order our world and determine the contours of a successful ministry or growth beyond measure. In some moments, to preach Christ is to gain. In some moments, preaching Christ will draw hundreds, even thousands, to the altar of faith, confessing their sins and seeking His forgiveness. Perhaps it is through the words of the preacher that this growth happens as evidence of the power of Christ.

Message Point 2: Preaching by Life or Death

Yes, and I will continue to rejoice, for I know that through your prayers and God's provision of the Spirit of Jesus Christ what has happened to me will turn out for my deliverance. I eagerly expect and hope that I will in no way be ashamed, but will have sufficient courage so that now as always Christ will be exalted in my body, whether by life or by death. For to me, to live is Christ and to die is gain (v. 19–22). But Paul also exhorts us that Christ will be preached by life or by death, by our presence or through our absence. To preach Christ is not merely to win lost souls to Christ but also to receive the world's "No!" Our ministries may struggle, our preaching may go unnoticed, our words may seemingly die on the vine. And so we are thrown back to this inexplicable truth, that Christ is exalted in our bodies, in the embodiment of our words and lives.

Message Point 3: Profundity of the Gospel

If I am to go on living in the body, this will mean fruitful labor for me. Yet what shall I choose? I do not know! I am torn between the two: I desire to depart and be with Christ, which is better by far; but it is more necessary for you that I remain in the body. Convinced of this, I know that I will remain, and I will continue with all of you for your progress and joy in the faith, so that through my being with you again your boasting in Christ Jesus will abound on account of me (v. 23–26). Paul highlights the profundity of the Gospel; it is not our word. It is not preached in our strength or certainty. It is not preached in the assurance that our lives are windows into righteousness. Instead, Paul's exhortation to the Philippians demonstrates a conviction that his life is torn between two yearnings, to be with Christ and serve Christ among his people. To preach Christ is not to live the perfect life but to inhabit the truth that our words are not ours, that our lives are not ours, and that this is a glorious gift. It is indeed cause to rejoice. Within Paul's assurance is also a communal promise: Paul belongs to Christ and he belongs to these people in whom he rejoices and abides. They are his, and he is theirs.

THAT'LL PREACH

There is a saying that goes like this, "People will forget what you said, people will forget what you did, but people will never forget how you made them feel." In the context of this passage, it is not so much our words or actions in ministry that will have impact on people. Those are definitely important aspects, but the true testimony comes from the experience of Jesus Christ and His saving grace. This is what the people listening to us or on the receiving end of our ministries should feel. The hope that comes from Jesus is what will stay with them through the good and bad times. So preach the Word and do good works so that people can experience Jesus!

CONCLUSION

In these exhortations, we can begin to inhabit a radical promise that the power of our words is not measured in re-tweets or blog hits, numbers in the seats, or "likes" on Facebook® . Also, Christ's power is also not measured by our separation from such vehicles of connection. If in the end, we recognize that the power lies not in our words but in the power of God, then Christ can be truly preached.

NOTES

Jesus' Humility and Exaltation

By Dr. Brian Bantum

Lesson Theme	Unit Theme	Scripture
Jesus' Humility and Exaltation	Jesus is Lord	Philippians 2:5–11

INTRODUCTION

In your relationships with one another, have the same mindset as Christ Jesus (v. 2:5). When considering the relationship between the Christians and the world, we often flee, resisting the temptations and unseemliness of the unbelieving world. Even more, these harsh judgments and postures of exclusivity mark our lives within communities of faith, the Church. And yet, Paul seems to exhort us to re-consider these relationships both beyond the walls of our churches and among our fellow sojourners in the faith in light of Christ's mindset toward humanity. But what is this mindset?

MESSAGE POINTS

Message Point 1: Jesus' Mindset

Who, being in very nature God, did not consider equality with God something to be used to his own advantage; rather, he made himself nothing by taking the very nature of a servant, being made in human likeness (v. 6–7). Paul's description of Christ draws us not into a simple mindset or an intellectual determination to be a certain way. Rather, Paul's description of Jesus' entrance into humanity displays that Jesus' mindset was a presence. The Incarnation was a presence that defied the very logic of what humanity thought was possible: that God could be seen, touched, and felt. This disorientation of a God in flesh leads us to another important observation. Not only did this mindset bring Christ into the presence of those He created and sustained, but He became present as a servant and as one who was subject to the nourishment of a young girl, Mary. Christ's presence was not one of physical dominance, of intellectual superiority, or of political prowess, though all of these were certainly possibilities latent within His divine body. No, Christ's power was demonstrated through His compassion, His service, His movement from spaces of destitution to places of power and back again. Christ's body was never apart from His mind. Christ's life was always the presence of mind.

Message Point 2: Jesus' Mentality Toward Human Suffering

And being found in appearance as a man, he humbled himself by becoming obedient to death—even death on a cross (v. 8)! This presence of mind brought Jesus not simply into the margins as a visitor, as one might be as a celebrity serving turkeys in the soup kitchens on Thanksgiving Day before returning home for a gourmet meal. No, this presence of mindtook Jesus only further into the depths of humanity's suffering. His obedience to love, to a desire to draw humanity out of its suffering, was not a feat of strength or power but of an abiding presence. Such presence existed even with death, with our own demise, our pain, our isolation, and our desolation. "Father, take this cup from me!" In this statement, Christ demonstrates the depths of humility. But what gives shape to this humility? It isn't a belief in His incapacity; nor is it a false declaration of what He can or cannot do. Jesus' humility was not seen in deflecting or minimizing His capacities but in His refusal to limit the benefits of His abundance.

There was no aspect of human life or longing or suffering that Christ was not willing to touch, to experience, or to endure. This is humility.

Message Point 3: Jesus' Magnificence

Therefore God exalted him to the highest place and gave him the name that is above every name, that at the name of Jesus every knee should bow, in heaven and on earth and under the earth, and every tongue acknowledge that Jesus Christ is Lord, to the glory of God the Father (v. 9–11).

THAT'LL PREACH

Humility is an important characteristic of Christ that people often misunderstand. Some people assume that if someone is humble, that they are quiet or introverted and might even consider them to be a doormat sort of person, easy to walk all over. If someone comes from a "humble" background, we might assume they do not have a lot of money or lack education. But this passage teaches us something different about humility in the way Jesus Christ embodies it. It is in the reversal of our understanding of humility that Christ is exalted. Therefore we should caution ourselves before we look down on those who we would consider humble in a negative sense.

CONCLUSION

Christ is exalted and declared to be the Son of God. However, this glory was always His. The honor was always due to Him. In His humility, Christ extended that glory and power into the depths of human existence so that we might be brought into the glory of communion and fellowship with God the Father, the Son, and the Holy Spirit. And what is it to have the mindset of Christ? Perhaps it is simply to ask of ourselves: How dare we withhold this presence from others? When looking at our neighbors or our neighborhood, will we see only where we cannot go, or will we have the mindset of Christ, who saw no space as unworthy of his presence?

NOTES

Gaining in Jesus Christ

Gaining in Jesus Christ

Lesson Theme	Unit Theme	Scripture
Gaining in Jesus Christ	Jesus is Lord	Philippians 3:7–11

INTRODUCTION

But whatever were gains to me I now consider loss for the sake of Christ (3:7). We all desire stability. In a culture where information is ubiquitous and where images of prosperity and fulfillment are so often tied to possessions, style, and bodies, it is easy to imagine that the health of our spiritual lives can also be measured by similar standards of success and happiness. And the desire for stability, for some semblance of certainty —to pay bills, to give our children a good education, to afford a small pleasure now and again—is something inherent to being human.

MESSAGE POINTS

Message Point 1: In Christ, Our Gains are Revealed to Be Losses.

We are not animals driven by natural instincts to forage, mate, and sleep. Endowed with intellect, love, desire, we humans can order our lives. As such, the possibility of disorder is often frightening, and in the Western world, to be resisted at all costs. Yet the standard of stability seems to change. The measure of order and faithfulness often shifts beneath our feet. We hope for the means to simply pay our bills, but once that is achieved, a vacation becomes a necessity. We hope for the possibility of transportation to get from one place to another, but eventually the cloth seats of a basic car do not seem to quite fit the bill. We yearn to eat well, have at least a few fruits and vegetables each week, but eventually these fruits do not seem to measure up to organic, local fruits. What does it mean to gain? Is there ever an end? The more we gain, often, the more we believe we securitize our lives, make certain what was once so uncertain. And yet our "gains" only bring us to ever more "necessities" and "standards" that we have not yet met.

Message Point 2: Righteousness of Contemporary Society

What is more, I consider everything a loss because of the surpassing worth of knowing Christ Jesus my Lord, for whose sake I have lost all things. I consider them garbage, that I may gain Christ and be found in him, not having a righteousness of my own that comes from the law, but that which is through faith in Christ—the righteousness that comes from God on the basis of faith (v. 8–9). The righteousness of our contemporary society is sometimes seen in our piety, our prayer time, or our Bible study. But too often the success of our lives is seen in patterns of life that are not measured by our devotion to Christ, but our participation in the systems of worship in our professions, our social circles, our neighborhoods.

Message Point 3: But What are These Systems of Gain, or Righteousness?

Paul considers them garbage. They are not the substance of what nourishes and sustains our bodies but that which is superfluous, extra, unnecessary, or no longer functions properly. Formerly our lives were oriented towards ways of life and patterns of consumption that were not essential to our life but were actually constituted by the waste of society, by habits and desires that had been cut away from what is best, by ways of life and standards that simply do not function as they should. And yet in our former lives we mistook these broken, cast-off systems to be the height of what it means to gain and be truly living.

Christ reveals our fixation on gain and success to be more about our control and desire for certainty than on Christ's power and love.

Message Point 4: To Know Christ

I want to know Christ—yes, to know the power of his resurrection and participation in his sufferings, becoming like him in his death, and so, somehow, attaining to the resurrection from the dead (v. 10–11). But to know Christ, even more to seek Him, is to not merely understand His life and work as a status we gain through belief or verbal affirmation. To know Christ is to participate in His life, to see our lives as too being extricated from the deceptions of success and happiness we have built for ourselves. No longer blind, we can see that what we considered gain was actually mistaking fat for meat, the cast-off bits of seed and stem for the nourishing heart of the fruit.

THAT'LL PREACH

Considering what it means to gain by biblical and worldly definitions brings to mind the Greek myth of King Midas. He was so consumed with greed and the desire for gain that he foolishly asked that everything he touched would turn to gold. While this made him happy when it applied to objects in his palace, he realized the gravity of the curse when he was unable to eat food or embrace his daughter. Some people use the phrase "Midas touch" to indicate good luck or flourishing but the story serves as a warning for those too focused on material gain.

CONCLUSION

To partake in this fruit, we may mourn the illusion we held on to so mightily. But in this mourning, we will come to find what it means to truly be nourished, to truly gain. In Christ, we find communion with our Creator and the possibility of true, fruitful lives with one another. To do this, we must also die, we must enter into that in-between space with Christ in His tomb so that we might emerge anew, perhaps unrecognizable to some, but with words of life and bound to one another in the Spirit of the Father and the Son. This is truly gain.

NOTES

Stand Firm

By Dr. Brian Bantum

Lesson Theme	Unit Theme	Scripture
Stand Firm	Jesus is Lord	Philippians 3:12–16

INTRODUCTION

Not that I have already obtained all this, or have already arrived at my goal, but I press on to take hold of that for which Christ Jesus took hold of me. Brothers and sisters, I do not consider myself yet to have taken hold of it (3:12–13). In Christ's life, death and resurrection, the fullness of life with God is made fully possible. In the entrance of the Word into the world, humanity's life is taken into God's very life. Being saved from the uncertainty of a life determined by our own determinations and desires, we can truly be in and with Christ. And yet, we remain within an interminable gap where we continue to listen as though we do not see, to grasp for doors, and feel for shifts in the ground beneath our feet. Though healed, we walk with the memory of our afflictions ingrained within our bodily lives and hearts. Somehow we do not always feel the newness of this promised resurrection. Our salvation and our walk in the promise is seemingly marred by the truth of our present imperfections.

MESSAGE POINTS

Message Point 1: Forgetting What is Behind

But one thing I do: Forgetting what is behind and straining toward what is ahead, I press on toward the goal to win the prize for which God has called me heavenward in Christ Jesus (vv. 13b–14). While the dried mud on our eyes reminds of what we once could not see, we must recall that now we can see. Forgetting what is behind is not to shut away the memory of our blindness, of our weaknesses, or of our anger or lust. But to forget is to resist those patterns of unfaithfulness that marked our lives in the dark.

Message Point 2: Pressing Forward

To press forward is to understand that we have traveled, that we have come from "a there" to "a here" not by our own strength or power but by the grace of Christ. In light of this, we press our bodies and lives into patterns of love for one another, into movements of mercy, and into embraces of forgiveness. Within our bodies we know and sense the tension of still living into this new body and reality. We struggle to acclimate to its tastes and desires. We struggle with the Spirit within us that seems to conflict with those patterns of desire that seem too familiar.

But those patterns are no longer who we are, for now we are not our own. Instead, we have been taken hold of and we press forward to return the embrace of the one who embraces us.

THAT'LL PREACH

Reviewing a timeline of Paul's life from his conversion reveals how he truly embodied this call to forget what is behind and press on toward the goal, no matter the circumstance. Paul left his life as a persecutor of believers behind (Acts 9) and focused on spreading the message of the Gospel. He was stoned and left for dead in Lystra (Acts 14:19–20). He was also imprisoned and then miraculously saved from the same place (Acts 16). He even survived a shipwreck and still managed to preach to the people of Malta (Acts 27–28). In all of these events, he kept his eyes on the prize promised in Jesus Christ.

CONCLUSION

All of us, then, who are mature should take such a view of things. And if on some point you think differently, God will also make that clear to you. Only let us live up to what we have already attained (vv. 15–16). Our maturity is not the attainment of perfection, but it is living into the reality that Christ has taken hold of us. Maturity resides in struggling to reciprocate God's embrace, living into it faithfully day by day, and letting the movement of Christ become our patterns. We should strive to let our words drip, however imperfectly, with mercy and humility. Perhaps others declare their holiness more boldly, but let the mature simply live in the holiness that lives in Christ. In this way, gaining the prize is to receive what is always radically and abundantly present to us in the Spirit.

NOTES

The Supremacy of Christ

Sylester Warsaw, Jr., Outreach Pastor

Lesson Theme	Unit Theme	Scripture
The Supremacy of Jesus Christ	Jesus is Lord	Colossians 1:15–20

INTRODUCTION

The French phenomenological philosopher Maurice Merleau-Ponty in perhaps his most famous book, "Phenomenology of Perception," argues that our perception plays a major role in our understanding of the physical world in which we live. To the unbeliever, and unfortunately for some Christians, this rings true because their understanding is based on what they believe subjectively. This is why our world is rocked when we have an encounter with the living Christ because mere human perception cannot grasp God's revelation. Philosophical beliefs have a bit of the truth whereas God's revelation is the truth because God is truth and this is the basis of Paul's argument here in this passage chosen for today.

MESSAGE POINTS

Message Point 1: Jesus, the Visible Revelation of the Invisible God

In verses 15–16, Paul argues for the uniqueness of the mystery of the God-head—the oneness of the God-head yet distinct in their function. Jesus is the personification of God, meaning He embodies the very nature and character of God. He was in the beginning with God. Jesus in the physical world is God's revelation to humanity; therefore, He is the one who defines it and not us. The uniqueness of the revelation of Jesus is that even though He was in the beginning and nothing was created without His union with God the Father, He is also the first to rise bodily from the dead after His incarnation and death. The text says in verse 16 that even the invisible things of Heaven were created by Him. The crux of our selected text for today is found in this 16th verse that says, "All things were created through Him and for Him." This tells us that you and I were created for Christ's purpose. We were created to be in relationship with Him worshiping Him in the beauty of holiness. This is what God's revelation in Jesus tells us: We are for His purpose and not our own as Frank Sinatra suggests in his song, "I did it my way."

Message Point 2: The Lordship of Jesus

Here in verses 17–18, Paul talks about the position of Jesus and His supremacy. Although Jesus is the second person of the God-head, everything is subjected to Him because "all things consists in Him." The whole of creation has His mark, and nothing created is without His mark. Although we humans have the ability to create, our creative ability is limited because we create from that which already exists and was created by Jesus; we don't have the ability to create from nothing. That which we create doesn't live but is manipulated from that which already exists. Verse 18 reveals Jesus' proper place, His preeminence as Lord of the Church. Historically and even today, there are those who try to downplay the Lordship of Jesus. There are those who try to put Him on the same plane as philosophical thinkers or movement leaders. They even dare to say there is more than one way to God the Father and that Jesus is not the only way. Don't believe the lie because Satan is still lying trying to steal God's glory. The Church exists because of who Jesus is and what He did on the Cross of Calvary. The blood of Christ was shed for humanity, and God does not care about one's blood type, ethnicity, or nationality. Jesus is God's revelation and the door to Him.

Message Point 3: Reconciliation Only in Christ

When we talk about the blood of Jesus, we are talking about sacrifice. Even the Old Covenant was always sealed with blood. Because of God's revelation of Himself as Jesus, Scripture tells us, God was in Christ reconciling the world back to Himself. Jesus came into a very violent world to violent people who had rejected the invisible God to reconcile humanity back to God with His life through the shedding of His blood. The message of the Gospel is summed up in verses 19–20: the Cross. The invisible God who created us in His image and likeness became visible, dwelt among us, and paid for us with His life. Who wouldn't serve a God like Him? He created us and bought us back. That tells us we have value in Christ Jesus—not because of who we are but because of who Christ is.

THAT'LL PREACH

"One day some teachers of religious law and Pharisees came to Jesus and said, "Teacher, we want you to show us a miraculous sign to prove your authority." But Jesus replied, "Only an evil, adulterous generation would demand a miraculous sign; but the only sign I will give them is the sign of the prophet Jonah. For as Jonah was in the belly of the great fish for three days and three nights, so will the Son of Man be in the heart of the earth for three days and three nights. "The people of Nineveh will stand up against this generation on judgment day and condemn it, for they repented of their sins at the preaching of Jonah. Now someone greater than Jonah is here—but you refuse to repent. The queen of Sheba will also stand up against this generation on judgment day and condemn it, for she came from a distant land to hear the wisdom of Solomon. Now someone greater than Solomon is here—but you refuse to listen." (Matthew 12:38–42, NLT) Scripture is clear: Jesus is SUPREME!

CONCLUSION

Philosophies may tingle the ear, but Jesus satisfies the heart. Whereas man has the ability to create, he creates from that which has already been created by and through Christ Jesus. Intellectualism and our own subjective realities cannot take the place of God's revelation, especially the revealed Christ in whom the sins of humanity were paid. Our limited creative ability cannot give life, but the Living Lord can give eternal life and that life is in Him alone. Jesus alone is Lord. He is the only way; not one of the ways. He reigns forever for He was in the beginning and all things were made for Him.

NOTES

Full Life in Christ

By Rev. Sylvester Warsaw, Jr., Outreach Pastor

Lesson Theme	Unit Theme	Scripture
Full Life in Christ	Jesus is Lord	Colossians 2:6–15 (NKJV)

INTRODUCTION

As a child growing up in the Church of the Black religious tradition, I remember clearly hearing the mature saints of God say, "You gotta know that you know" meaning you had to know Christ for yourself and not what someone told you about Him. They would also say that when we stand before Jesus, we can't ask anyone—not even the preacher—to plead our case, for that person has his or her own case to plead. Jeremiah, as inspired by God, penned these words in Jeremiah 31:31–34, *"Behold, the days are coming, says the LORD, when I will make a new covenant with the house of Judah—not according to the covenant that I made with their fathers in the day that I took them by the hand to lead them out of the land of Egypt, My covenant which they broke, though, I was a husband to them, says the LORD. But this is the covenant that I will make with the house of Israel after those days, says the LORD; I will put My law in their minds, and write it on their hearts; and I will be their God, and they shall be My people. No more shall every man teach his neighbor, and every man his brother, saying, 'Know the LORD,' for they all shall know Me, from the least of them to the greatest of them, says the LORD. For I will forgive their iniquity, and their sin I will remember no more."*

MESSAGE POINTS

Message Point 1: Christ the Solid Rock

A songwriter wrote, "On Christ the solid rock I stand. All other ground is sinking sand." This songwriter captures the essence of what Paul is conveying in this letter to the Colossians in verses 6–7 as well as what Psalm 127:1 tells us: "Unless the LORD builds a house, They labor in vain who build it; Unless the LORD guards the city, The watchman stays awake in vain." These two verses clearly state that we must hunger and thirst after Jesus, the author and finisher of our faith. This verse tells you and I as children of God that we are supposed to grow in the faith. We grow by seeking His face, falling in love with Him as He sups with us and we with Him. We are told that we must have the attitude of thanksgiving. We are to be thankful for what Christ did that gives us the opportunity to be in Him. Philosophy tells us that we have to find our own way; whereas, Jesus says He is the way the truth and the life and that we are never alone in Him.

Message Point 2: False Teachers

Many well-meaning Christians sitting in the pews are being and have been led astray because they refuse to grow in the grace and knowledge of Christ. Many have itching ears and only want to hear that which makes them feel good. Many want the easy way out without allowing Christ to take them through something, giving them a testimony that glorifies and honors Him. Because I am an American, I can say that many Americans have this sense of entitlement. This ungodly teaching is permeating our houses of worship. Verses 8–10 warn the body of Christ strongly about worldly teaching and the teachings of man. The Word of God cleanses us from unrighteousness.

The growth in this does not feel good because the flesh does not want to die. God does not want us to have a lack of knowledge, but instead, He wants us to have Godly knowledge that is rooted in Him as we encounter and experience Him. We have everything we need and can ever want in Christ Jesus.

Message Point 3: Salvation in Christ

Circumcision of males was major within the Jewish culture for identity purposes. Every male child, even Jesus, had to be circumcised on the eighth day after his birth. Paul, in verses 11 through 15, is not talking about a physical circumcision of the male foreskin at 8 days old but, he is talking about spiritual circumcision of the heart that only Christ can perform. Paul is talking about repentance of the heart and not with the lips. For it is the heart that God looks at for where He wants to dwell. Salvation is not earned by what we do but what Christ not only did on Calvary's Cross but also in His rising from the dead. Our acceptance of God's redemptive act of salvation through Jesus Christ is His work and His work alone. Our decision to accept Christ and to be baptized is our outward confession of what has taken place inside. Making a decision to follow Christ is proclaiming that you are not willing to follow the ways of this world order; even though we are in this world, we are not of this world. Our allegiance is to God and our aim is to follow the path He has set for us.

THAT'LL PREACH

"Anyone who listens to my teaching and follows it is wise, like a person who builds a house on solid rock. Though the rain comes in torrents and the floodwaters rise and the winds beat against that house, it won't collapse because it is built on bedrock. But anyone who hears my teaching and doesn't obey it is foolish, like a person who builds a house on sand. When the rains and floods come and the winds beat against that house, it will collapse with a mighty crash" (Matthew 7:24–27, NLT).

The parable of the wise and foolish builders begs the question, what is your life built on? False teachings? Your own strength? Storms will come, but only Jesus is our solid rock!

CONCLUSION

Just as the centurion after the death of Jesus recognized and confessed that Jesus is the Son of God, we must all recognize that Jesus is Lord. More importantly, we the body of Christ must know that He is Lord and the life He gives us must reflect, glorify, and honor Him. Repentance is not a free ticket to keep sinning because God forgives us of our sins, but repentance means we've made a conscious decision to follow Him. God wants to sanctify us through the indwelling presence of the Holy Spirit. Cleansing is the work of the Holy Spirit. "What can wash away my sins? Nothing but the blood of Jesus." What sacrifice are you willing to make to experience the fullness of Christ Jesus working in this life He has given you? God is not interested in our lip service but what is in our heart. Is your all on the altar of sacrifice laid; your heart does the Spirit control? You know if the Spirit of God controls your life. Now is the day of surrender.

NOTES

New Clothes

By Tawanna Boyd

Lesson Theme	Unit Theme	Scripture
Clothed with Christ	Jesus is Lord	Colossians 3:5–17

INTRODUCTION

Paul is clear that as believers in Christ we must take off our old ways and habits that were taught and nurtured by a selfish world. As Christians, we have and continue to experience a metamorphosis by which our nakedness or authentic selves are being redressed in the garments and likeness of Christ. This is not simply for our benefit but for the purpose of evidencing God's presence and reign through our thanksgiving, witness, and example.

MESSAGE POINTS

Message Point 1: Are You Willing to Change Clothes? (v. 5–9)

- One must be willing to take off the old clothes in order to put on new clothes. We must be willing to let go of things and ways that do not illustrate that we have had an encounter with Christ. If we try putting on new clothes on top of old clothes:
    - The new clothes don't smell new. It may be obvious that you have on new clothes, but, if nothing else, the smell of the old clothes is a distraction to the new clothes and draws even more attention to the old clothes underneath.
    - To put new clothes on top of old clothes, you have to buy clothes that are really too big, don't fit, and may even give the impression that you are wearing clothes meant for someone else.
- We must discard the old things that previously governed our lives, such as money, careers, and popularity.
    - We must be willing to discard the old clothes.
    - We have to get rid of our old selfish ways and bad habits that caused us to be far away from Christ in the first place.
- We must look to a new authority for living. No longer do we look to the world as the authority for life, but as Christians, Christ must be that authority.

Message Point 2: Now That You Have Decided to Put on New Clothes (v. 10–11)

- Making the decision to take off your clothes and put on some new clothes is just the beginning, but we must actually put the new clothes on. When we put on the new clothes of Christ, the evidence will show in our new Christ-like attitudes.
- Don't let your new clothes go to your head. Be diligent in seeking the Lord and the Lord's ways, being ever mindful that your new clothes are a gift from God.

Message Point 3: Sportin' Your New Outfit (v. 12–17)

- It does you no good to wear your new clothes with an old attitude. Let your relationship with others reflect your consciousness of God's love and grace.
- Share your new clothes story. Help others to get a new set of clothes.
- Keep your new clothes looking like new by being intentional about engaging the means of grace such as Bible study, prayer, worship, praise, and fellowship.

THAT'LL PREACH

"What you wear is how you present yourself to the world, especially today, when human contacts are so quick. Fashion is instant language." —Miuccia Prada

While the founder and head designer of the luxury brand, Prada, was talking about the clothes we wear on our bodies, her advice could also apply to our new clothes in Christ. The impact Jesus has had on our lives should be evident as soon as we walk into a room. We do not even need to speak because the presence is already all over us. Believers have access to an instant language of peace, joy, and grace in the Spirit thanks to the sacrifice of Jesus.

CONCLUSION

As Christians, we have to be intentional about how we wear and care for our new garments given as a gift from Jesus Christ. Through prayer, Bible study, fellowship, and practice we must keep our Christian garment of Christ-likeness in good shape. We do this not simply for our own sake or to draw attention to ourselves, but we do this that it might show evidence of the goodness, grace, and the love of God. We do it so that God may be glorified.

NOTES

Be Ready: God Wants to Use You

By Pastor Tawanna Boy

Lesson Theme	Unit Theme	Scripture
Spiritual Disciplines for New Life	Jesus is Lord	Colossians 4:2–6

INTRODUCTION

To reach mastery level of a given skill, one must put great energy and effort into developing that skill. So it is with Christians. To grow in spiritual strength and fortitude, we must put much energy and effort into spiritual disciplines (prayer, study, worship, fellowship, etc.). Although God is gracious, we have responsibility in our spiritual development both as individuals and as the body of Christ.

MESSAGE POINTS

Message Point 1: The Importance of Prayer (v. 2–4)

Prayer is the connection to the power source of God by which we are able to stand for God. Prayer is a vehicle by which we intentionally seek God. It is important that prayer be done in the spirit of community. Be careful what you pray for. Prayer should not be done out of selfishness (Ephesians 6:19). Prayer is not to be used to summon God to advance our personal agendas but for strengthening, nurturing, and the revealing of God's agenda. Prayer not only involves speaking, but it also involves listening. Remember God's authority over life. Use prayer as a means of being or getting prepared for the great work of spreading the Good News.

Message Point 2: Look for Opportunity (When Opportunity Knocks)

Remember God is the God of all creation and that He also cares for the lost. Jesus teaches about the shepherd who would leave his flock in search for the one lost sheep as well as the Good Shepherd who has "other sheep" not of this fold. (Luke 15 1–7, John 11:16). Live life expecting God to use you to reveal Himself or be a blessing to someone else.

Message Point 3: Always be On Duty

We are called to always be on duty, and we must make every effort to be our best at all times. We can only be our best for God when we are in communion with Him through spiritual disciplines. We need to be in communion with God so that even our everyday speech and behavior will reflect what God has revealed to us in our hearts.

THAT'LL PREACH

Sometimes we do not know how or what to pray for. But it is really as easy as **ABCD**! Next time you pray, consider including the following: **Adoration**, praise God for all that He has done for you and just for who He is (Psalm 150:1-2); **Blessings**, thank God for the ways in which God has supplied your needs and the needs of those around you, no blessing is too small to thank God for (1 Thess. 5:18); **Confession**, although God already knows everything we do, say, and feel, take the opportunity to bear yourself before the Lord trusting that He is willing and just to forgive (1 John 1:9); **Desires**, end your prayer time asking God for what you need and what aligns with His will (Psalm 37:4).

CONCLUSION

To be fervent and effectual in our Christian walk, we must engage in spiritual disciplines both privately and in community. As a spiritual discipline, prayer is essential and important. In addition, the perspective from which we engage in it is critical. Prayer is a vehicle by which God communicates with us so that we may have revelation of God's desire for our lives. That includes sharing our faith with others who may then see the evidence of God and embrace His desire for their own lives. It is not our job to judge who we should share our faith with but to consistently live in way that is reflective of God's presence and mercy. We must always let our light shine for all to see.

NOTES

March 5, 2023

Hope for Final Justice

By Dr. Kevin Hrebik

Lesson Theme	**Unit Theme**	**Scripture**
Daniel's Vision of Change	Beyond the Present Time	Daniel 7:9–14

INTRODUCTION

Daniel is the most quoted book in the New Testament with the most fulfilled prophesies. Daniel wrote from exile in Babylon (1:21; 10:1; 7:1). God favored Daniel with the gift of interpreting dreams (6:28).

MESSAGE POINTS

Message Point 1: Daniel's Dream

The passage starts in middle of Daniel writing down his dream (see 7:2–8). The prior portion of dream has four winds and four "beasts." The fourth beast had 10 horns, which indicated 10 powers. One of the horns eventually supplants three. The passage following interprets the dream (7:17–28).

In this Heavenly courtroom scene, the Ancient of Days sits on judgment throne. The throne is ablaze with flaming wheels, reminding readers that our God is "a consuming fire" (Deuteronomy 4:24). There are countless celestial beings as witnesses (v. 10). Books for judgment of beasts and the wicked are opened (Revelation 20:12).

Message Point 2: Fourth Beast Destroyed (v. 11)

Death silences boasting mouth of "little horn" (7:8). The other horns and beasts' had their power removed but their destruction postponed (v. 12). Most believe beasts are earth's imperial superpowers with the fourth beast being the antichrist (2 Thessalonians 2:3–4).

Message Point 3: Son of man comes with clouds (v. 13; Exodus 16:10; Psalm 104:3; Isaiah 19:1; Nahum 1:3)

Jesus quotes Daniel's words regarding his second coming (Matthew 24:30, 26:64; Mark 13:26) in which the Son of Man is given dominion, glory, kingdom (v. 14). This is the same authority Jesus cites in Great Commission (Matthew 28:18). Daniel foresees Jesus' future eternal kingdom where "every knee shall bow" (Isaiah 45:23; Romans 14:11; Philippians 2:10). This message is indeed good news for those who have suffered under the rule of empire.

THAT'LL PREACH

Throughout his narrative, Daniel often encountered dreams, both his own and those of the king of the Empire where he was in exile. In Daniel 2, he interprets Nebuchadnezzar's dream of a statue made of different materials. God reveals the meaning of this dream to Daniel, who is able to gain an audience before Nebuchadnezzar and offer an interpretation where the wise men could not. Because of this, the king honors Daniel. Today's passage focuses on a dream that Daniel had that deeply disturbed him, "my spirit was troubled within me, and the visions of my head terrified me." (Daniel 7:15) But Daniel still had faith in God. Sometimes God reveals something challenging to us and we must pray to understand how to move forward. Daniel closes the chapter with these words, "As for me, Daniel, my thoughts greatly terrified me, and my face turned pale; but I kept the matter in my mind." (Daniel 7:28)

CONCLUSION

Noting that New Testament eschatology is based heavily in Daniel shows how God used ancient prophet in exile to speak future hope to all believers. It might not have made sense to Daniel then, but we thank God for his obedience to write it all down for our benefit.

NOTES

A Prose Prayer of Penitence

By Dr. Kevin Hrebik

Lesson Theme	Unit Theme	Scripture
Daniel's Prayer	Beyond the Present Time	Daniel 9:4b–14

INTRODUCTION

- With the arrival of Cyrus on the scene in 538 B.C., Daniel knows that Israel's 70-year exile in Babylon is nearly over.
- Daniel recognizes the timing and details from Isaiah's and Jeremiah's prophecies (Isaiah 44:28; 45:1–2, 4, 13; Jeremiah 25:11–12; 29:10).
- Daniel offers a prayer that the God who keeps His covenants (v. 4b) will restore His people to their land and city, as the prophets foretold.

MESSAGE POINTS

Message Point 1: Daniel's Great Prayer (v. 4b-19) Daniel prepares himself for a solemn prayer (v. 3).
He turns his face toward God and Jerusalem. He fasts, mourns, and wears sackcloth. He responds in this way based on his understanding of the words of the prophet Jeremiah. To be a prophet means to be a mediator between God and God's people. The task is not always comfortable. It can take a physical and emotional toll. It is a callign that should not be taken lightly.

Message Point 2: Daniel addresses God in the first person, and includes himself (vv. 4–8).
His salutation proclaims God's transcendence and His unchanging mercy (v. 4b).He acknowledges Israel's iniquity and wickedness and their violating God's righteous precepts and judgments (v. 5). He confesses Israel's ignoring (and shedding the innocent blood) of God's prophets (v. 6). He confesses their utter shame and guilt, which the entire world has witnessed and brought reproach onto God's nation and people (vv. 7-8). The prophet does not consider themselves to be above anyone else. They are part of the people they represent.

Message Point 3: Daniel addresses God in the third person, as if he's delivering a sermon (vv. 9–14).
He testifies to God's well known mercy and forgiveness (v. 9). He expresses in one sentence the essence of both Old and New Testaments. By rejecting God's laws, they also rejected His promises (v. 10). Israel has worked hard to earn God's punishment; a just God cannot overlook such egregious sins (v. 11). The only recourse was what Daniel was doing; throwing himself on the mercy of God's court (vv. 12–14). The prophet communicates with God and the people, praying not only for God's merciful repsonse but for the people to respond with reprentance.

THAT'LL PREACH

Daniel's prayer of penitence in chapter 9 exhibits what psychologists identify as the three components of a sincere apology. These include expressing regret, "we have sinned and done wrong, acted wickedly and rebelled, turning aside from your commandments and ordinances. We have not listened to your servants the prophets, who spoke in your name to our kings, our princes, and our ancestors, and to all the people of the land." (vv. 5–6); accepting responsibility, "Righteousness is on your side, O Lord, but open shame, as at this day, falls on us" (v. 7); and, of course, asking for forgiveness, "O Lord, hear; O Lord, forgive; O Lord, listen and act and do not delay! For your own sake, O my God, because your city and your people bear your name!" (v.19) This prayer for forgiveness shows the genuine relationship between God and God's people, mediated by the prophets.

CONCLUSION

- Daniel does not justify Israel's sins; he holds God blameless for His judgment against the nation.
- The only hope for Israel will be found in God's mercy and grace, which Daniel clung to in faith. That is a model prayer for all ages and the only doorway for redemption and restoration.

NOTES

March 19, 2023

Daniel Receives a Vision

By Dr. Kevin Hrebik

Lesson Theme	Unit Theme	Scripture
Gabriel's Interpretation	Beyond the Present Time	Daniel 8:19–26

INTRODUCTION

- Daniel's vision here is added to his dream in chapter 7. In a rare theophany (a visible manifestation to humankind of God), God instructs the angel Gabriel to deliver the vision to Daniel (v. 16).
- The vision details events pertaining to the coming destruction and desecration committed by Antiochus IV Epiphanes in 168–167 BC; they also parallel and prototype a future antichrist.

MESSAGE POINTS

Message Point 1: The "Last End of the Indignation" (v. 19)

- The indignation is Epiphanes' destruction, where tens of thousands were masacared, and the temple desecrated by the setting up of a statue of Zeus and sacrificing pigs on altar (see also Daniel 8:13; 9:27; 11:31; 12:11).
- The appointed "end" can be for any end; the aforementioned example, and the ultimate end times (Habakkuk 2:3; Daniel 10:14; 11:27, 35). God sees the evil that is happening in the power. People in power taking advantage and mocking God's holiness. But God will one day bring everything into account.

Message Point 2: Animals representing earthly kings and kingdoms (v. 20–22)

- In this vision there was a two-horned ram that represented the empires of Media and Persia, which were overtaken by a one-horned he-goat—Greece, led by Alexander the Great (see Daniel 8:3, 5, 7).
- Although he gains this great victory, Alexander dies prematurely, and his four generals divide his kingdom.

Message Point 3: Antiochus IV Epiphanes, son of one of the four generals, Seleucus III, invades Judea and crushes Jerusalem in 168-167 B.C. (vv. 23–24).

- Epiphanes is a blasphemer, naming himself "the Illustrious God." He puts an end to sacrifices, (8:11), outlaws Judaism, and expects Israelites to bow down to Zeus. Epiphanes is an example of an imperial force anointed by Satan, the great deceiver (Genesis 3:13; John 8:44; Revelation 12:9).
- In the end, all will bow before God and be judged (Romans 14:11; Hebrews 9:27).

Message Point 4: Daniel is told to seal up, to protect the vision, for the appointed time was in the future (v. 26).

- This passage runs parallel to the eschatological "end times" (see Daniel 10:14; 11:27, 35).
- In the same way, Jesus told some (including demons) not to reveal His identity before His time (Matthew 8:9; Mark 1:34; 13:32–33; Luke 4:41).

THAT'LL PREACH

The instructions given to Daniel to seal up the vision until the appointed time is reminiscent of creating a time capsule. Time capsules are often made by graduating classes in different levels of schooling. A time capsule usually includes photos, videos, and momentos of the current time. They are usually sealed and buried for anywhere from five to fifty years. Looking back at the contents of the time capsule reminds the group of how life was at that time and what goals and aspirations they might have had for themselves. This activity can reveal both what has changed and what has remained consistent over the span of many years. Daniels vision was for a later time but we have seen the manifestations of empire described in it repeated throughout history. When we look back on the history of the Church five, ten, even fifty years from now, what will be said?

CONCLUSION

Taking Caution—Prophetic literature, especially apocalyptic, is extremely hard to decipher and assign to specific events in history. Extreme caution must be used to prevent individual embarrassment as well as that of the entire Church.

Trust in What's to Come—Ultimately, even though Satan has the ability to destroy the visible elements of the church and God's holy places, all believers take hope in the future eternal Jerusalem and Temple, which can never be harmed, and the time when all evil will be completely and permanently destroyed (Revelation 20:10, 14).

NOTES

March 26, 2023

A Meal to Remember

By Dr. Kevin Hrebik

Lesson Theme	**Unit Theme**	**Scripture**
The Lord's Supper	Beyond the Present Time	Luke 22:14–30

INTRODUCTION

- Jesus instructs disciples to prepare for upcoming Passover (v. 1, 8).
- Mark and Luke mention sacrificed lamb (v. 7; Mark 14:12).
- Passover is one day, Nisan 15, starts on first day of Feast of Unleavened Bread, which lasts a week (Nisan 15–21).
- Millions of pilgrims come each year to Jerusalem for Passover, but Jesus will change the annual celebration forever (1 Corinthians 5:7).

MESSAGE POINTS

Message Point 1: Jesus Institutes Lord's Supper

- As instructed, disciples gather in the upper room (Gk., *katalyma*) in a home.
- Jesus expresses His strong feelings with strong words.
  - He will participate but never again until His kingdom comes (v. 16, 18).
  - New Testament believers still await the coming kingdom.
- Jesus gives thanks with both cup and bread (Gk., *eucharisteo*)
  - Two cups refer to second and third cups in traditional four-cup Passover (v. 17, 20).
  - The Gospel of Luke alone has bread/body "given for you" and wine/blood "shed for you" (v. 20).

Message Point 2: Judas, a quarrel, and a teaching

- Judas is present for the first part of meal, showing how the enemy can infiltrate and break bread with true disciples (v. 21).
- Even though events are divinely ordained, Judas is still responsible for Jesus' betrayal (v. 22).
- Disciples quarrel over who is greatest and who will sit closest to Jesus (v. 24).
- Jesus uses the occasion to teach and encourage disciples.
  - He reminds them about secular rulers who abuse absolute authority, inflicting injustice and cruelty while giving themselves grandiose titles—a timeless warning about worldly greatness (v. 25).

- Disciples are subtly reminded about vicious despots, such as Antiochus IV Epiphanes.
- In the kingdom of God, the greatest is the greatest servant (v. 26).
- In the end, those who endure will be well rewarded (v. 28–30).

THAT'LL PREACH

The Gospel of Luke features several instances of Jesus teaching a lesson while sharing a meal, including The Last Supper. There are ten altogether, allow me to highlight three more examples. Jesus had a banquet at Levi's house with tax collectors and sinners to show that He did not come to call the righteous, but sinners to repentance (Luke 5:27–39). Jesus experienced the hospitality of both Mary and Martha, acknowledging that the former had chosen better to sit at His feet and learn from Him rather than be pre-occupied with service (Luke 10:38–42). Jesus revealed Himself to the believers gathered at Emaus in the breaking of bread after His Resurrection (Luke 24:13–35). Meals are obviously an important teaching tool for Jesus and should continue to be among our practices as believers today.

CONCLUSION

- Passover presented the perfect symbolism for Christ's Passion—each event informs the other.
- The Lord's Supper is only one of two sacraments Jesus instituted—because of it, "No meal among disciples is just a meal, because no loaf is just bread, no cup is just wine," in Fred Craddock's words.
- The Lord's Supper looks back to the original events in Egypt, and forward tothe messianic marriage supper of the Lamb.

Source: Craddock, Fred. *Luke: Interpretation: A Bible Commentary for Teaching and Preaching.* Louisville, KY. Westminster John Knox Press, 2009. p. 255.

NOTES

The Lord Has Risen Indeed

By Dr. Moussa Coulibaly

Lesson Theme	Unit Theme	Scripture
The Lord Has Risen Indeed!	Beyond the Present Time	Luke 24:13–21, 28–35

INTRODUCTION

People sometimes worry about situations that have already been resolved. This can come from their predisposition toward the contrary of their own expectation. Unbelief can lead a person to despair and breed forgetfulness. A troubled spirit lacks the sharpness of mind to apprehend events and circumstances that are favorable.

The narrative of the Emmaus road presents the picture of two disciples confused about the events of Jesus' death and the news of the empty tomb. The Lord used appearances, Scripture explanation, and familiar actions to convince them that He has risen from the dead. It is the repeated testimony of Jesus' appearances that convince both the two disciples and others of the Resurrection.

MESSAGE POINTS

Message Point 1: The unrecognized companionship of Jesus (vv. 13–21)

Disturbed by the report of the women concerning the empty tomb of Jesus, two disciples on the road of Emmaus were discussing it in attempts to solve the puzzle (vv. 13, 14). Then Jesus Himself came and walked along with them (v. 15). He knew the confusion in their minds that would prevent them from recognizing Him (v. 16). As a compassionate Lord, He wanted to relieve them of the burden they bore and bring light into their troubled minds. Jesus therefore engaged in an interaction with them. His questions were directed to unearth the ailing part of their logic (vv. 17, 19a).

The disciples' perspectives of the events blur their way of seeing and analyzing things. To them, their hope in a Messiah who would deliver them from Roman subjection was forfeited by the death of Jesus. They saw their only reference of joy in the past. Jesus was a prophet powerful in word and deed. The disciples needed to project themselves into the future as individuals and as a nation. Unfortunately their hope died in the past (vv. 19b, 21). They could not appraise the brightness of the present that would link them to the future. However Jesus, their companion, was not only a powerful testimony of the days gone by but also of the light in the present ushering them into a hopeful future. The tomb was not an end; it was a transit.

Message Point 2: The revelation of the resurrected Jesus (vv. 28–35)

Jesus wanted to continue His journey (v. 28), but the disciples desired to have Him as their guest. Moreover, it was late, and the traditional hospitality would not allow them to let their friend continue His way by night (v. 29). Once in their home, the disciples set the table for dinner. From there, the roles were reversed; the guest blessed the meal, broke the bread, and began to share (v. 30). Something familiar caught the attention of the two disciples, and they recognized their famous companion. The man who joined them on the road was Jesus. However, they did not have the time to come back from their surprise and excitement before Jesus vanished (v. 31). Having come to their senses, they realized they'd neglected a hint. Their hearts burned within them when Jesus explained the Scriptures (v. 32).

The discovery they made motivated them to go back to Jerusalem in spite of the late hour to share their wonderful experience with the other disciples (v. 33). They were welcomed with similar news: The Lord had risen and appeared to Simon (v. 34). The two disciples' experience would serve to confirm what the others knew based on their encounters with the living Savior (v. 35).

THAT'LL PREACH

Viral videos of soldiers returning home and reuniting with their families inevitably tug at the heartstrings. There is an element of surprise and even confusion when the service person arrives or hides at their loved one's school, job, or even hiding in a mascot suit at a sporting event. Once they are revealed, there is usually an overflow of tears and embraces after the initial shock. Even pets of service people show great joy in these reunions! Imagine how overcome the followers of Jesus must have been when they realized that He had truly risen and had not only walked with them along the road to Emmaus, but also shared a meal with them. No wonder they were so excited to share!

CONCLUSION

The state of confusion prevents us from recognizing the works of God in our lives. However, the Lord is ever ready to be our companion and walk with us through our sorrows and despair. He will patiently assist and guide us toward understanding of His wonders performed in our lives. He always gives us a testimony to share with other brethren to strengthen them as they also encourage us with their own testimonies.

NOTES

April 9, 2023

The Lord Appears

By Dr. Moussa Coulibaly

Lesson Theme	Unit Theme	Scripture
The Lord Appears	Beyond the Present Time	Luke 24:36–53

INTRODUCTION

God is ever ready to give us a clear understanding of what is happening when we are in doubt. When our minds wander in an attempt to reconstruct some puzzling issue or to ascertain the wonders of God, He has His ways to lead us to true assurance and, by that, cast doubt aside.

The disciples in the upper room were excited at the prospect of Jesus' Resurrection after His appearances to some of them. However they needed to check to be sure that it was really Him and not His ghost. Unless they had a clear assurance, they would not be able to bear witness. A doubting mind will always be hesitant in its endeavors.

MESSAGE POINTS

Message Point 1: Convincing evidences of the Resurrection of Jesus (vv. 36–43)

Jesus' appearance in the upper room during the gathering of the disciples aimed to provide vivid proof to all of them that He was alive. He assured them of the peace they needed most (v. 36) because they were frightened, thinking they had seen a ghost (v. 37). The Lord reassured them and asked them to check for themselves to be sure that He was alive (vv. 38, 39).

To give them a final convincing assurance of His bodily Resurrection, Jesus asked for food to eat. They gave Him broiled fish that He ate in their presence (vv. 42, 43). When they were finally convinced, Jesus could then explain though Scripture all of the events they had been unable to understand. He then set the stage for the mission ahead of them. On the Emmaus road, Jesus explained the Scriptures before eating. Here, He ate before explaining the Scriptures.

Message Point 2: Preparation for the future mission after Jesus (vv. 44–49)

Jesus reminds the disciples of His interactions with them before His death. He told them that He had come to fulfill the Scriptures and that what was written concerning Him would come true (v. 44). After this, He opened their minds to a disposition of heart that would enable them to understand the meaning of the Scriptures (v. 45). Jesus explained the suffering, death and Resurrection of Christ from the dead. As a result, repentance and forgiveness of sins had to be preached to all nations, with Jerusalem as the launching place for this (46, 47). It was important for Jesus to convince the disciples of His Resurrection because they were the chosen witnesses for these things. They had observed His death, and they needed to see the complete picture of the salvation story by witnessing the Resurrection (v. 48). Although, they were already on a mission to proclaim what they had seen, they needed to be equipped by God for the task ahead. They were therefore asked to wait for equipment of power through the Holy Spirit before starting their work (v. 49).

Message Point 3: The ascension of Jesus (vv. 50–53)

After convincing the disciples of His Resurrection and giving them their missions, Jesus was ready to leave. He then led them to Bethany and gave them His final blessing. Then, overcoming the law of gravity, He departed from them into heaven (vv. 50, 51). They worshiped Him as their Lord and returned to Jerusalem to wait for the promise He made to them. While waiting, they spent their time praising God (vv. 52, 53).

THAT'LL PREACH

How you ever heard of Ripley's Believe It or Not? Ripley's Believe It or Not! is an American franchise founded by Robert Ripley, which deals in bizarre events and items so strange and unusual that readers might question the claims. Originally a newspaper panel, the Believe It or Not feature proved popular and was later adapted into a wide variety of formats, including radio, television, comic books, a chain of museums and a book series. The Ripley collection includes 20,000 photographs, 30,000 artifacts and more than 100,000 cartoon panels. Often people need to see evidence to believe a bizarre event. The disciples were so astounded that Jesus had resurrected, they needed to touch His scars and see Him eat before they could even begin to comprehend this marvelous occurrence!

Source: Wikipedia, Ripley's Believe It or Not!, https://en.wikipedia.org/wiki/Ripley%27s_Believe_It_or_Not!

CONCLUSION

A troubled and confused spirit cannot see beyond the present circumstances. Therefore, a confused person cannot be useful in the task he may be given to perform. Jesus, knowing that, took time to convince His disciples and give them an assurance of His Resurrection. When their trouble and confusion dissipated, Jesus then presented them the mission of evangelizing to the world.

If we are also troubled and confused, we need assurance and hope from the Lord before we can be useful and faithfully accomplish whatever He has asked us to do.

NOTES

The Holy Spirit's Power Transforms the World

By Elder Aaron O. Howard

Lesson Theme	Unit Theme	Scripture
The Holy Spirit Comes	Beyond the Present Time	Acts 2:1–13

INTRODUCTION

In Acts 2, Luke details a momentous event whose reverberations are still being felt daily across the world through the lives of Christians like Reinhart Bonnke. On the Day of Pentecost, Christ's promise that He would send the Holy Spirit was fulfilled. Even now, the Gospel continues to be preached across the globe, and the power of the Holy Spirit ensures the continuation of this mission. Through this power, people experience miracles, signs, and wonders that bring glory to Jesus Christ, and all over the world the church testifies that God's power is greater than any other. We must seek to continually be filled with the Holy Spirit so that Jesus Christ will be glorified in the lives of our churches, our communities, and the world.

MESSAGE POINTS

Message Point 1: The Holy Spirit is power (Acts 2:1–4)

The Holy Spirit reveals His supernatural power. When the 120 disciples were gathered together in unity, the Holy Spirit fell on them, and He manifested himself as tongues of fire. Everyone in the room was filled with the Holy Spirit and spoke in other tongues by the power of the Spirit.

The Holy Spirit causes us to experience the divine power of God in astonishing and awe-inspiring ways. Whether through healing, prophecy, exorcism, or even resurrection of the dead, the Holy Spirit announces that God is present in the midst of His people. These supernatural manifestations result in God giving the glory (1 Corinthians 14:25), and the church is strengthened and renewed.

Message Point 2: The Holy Spirit transforms the world (Acts 2:5–13)

The church, in its focus on the personal experience of being baptized in the Holy Spirit, often neglects the global implications of being filled with the Spirit. We are filled with the Holy Spirit to be witnesses, first to our own communities and then eventually to the world. The Holy Spirit is given so that we will become bold in proclaiming the Word of God. We are not merely to enjoy praising God within the walls of our churches, but we are to go out and spread the Gospel of Jesus Christ beyond the confines of the church sanctuary.

The Scriptures undergird this principle by letting us know that people from all over the world heard the gospel in their own tongue. The people said, "We hear them in our own tongues speaking of the mighty deeds of God" (Acts 2:11, NASB). This means that the Holy Spirit broke through cultural and geographic boundaries so that all could experience the Gospel.

THAT'LL PREACH

Evangelist Reinhart Bonnke* is a preacher who has seen God do great things in Africa through the power of the Holy Spirit. God gave him a vision that the continent of Africa would be washed in the blood of Jesus. Since that vision many years ago, Bonnke has had as many as 1.6 million African people in attendance at one service! He has documented more than 55 million decisions to accept Christ since he has been in ministry. Through the power of the Holy Spirit, Bonnke has experienced the greater works that Jesus promised we would do (John 14:12).

***Source:** CFAN: Christ for All Nations. Evangelist Reinhard Bonnke. http://www.us.cfan.org/Reinhard-Bonnke- Biography.aspx (accessed April 23, 2012)

CONCLUSION

The Holy Spirit enables us to transcend cultural, geographic, and societal boundaries to take the Gospel message to everyone who needs to hear it. We are empowered by the Holy Spirit to reclaim our inner-city communities which have been besieged by poverty, negligence, and criminal activity. We are empowered to look beyond our four walls to become missionary minded so that the whole world is able to hear the Gospel of Jesus Christ. By being filled with the Spirit, the Gospel becomes available to the whole world. The power that is available to men of God like Reinhart Bonnke is available to us all.

NOTES

Rejoicing at Christ's Return

By Elder Aaron O. Howard

Lesson Theme	Unit Theme	Scripture
Living with Hope	Beyond the Present Time	1 Thessalonians 4:13–5:11

INTRODUCTION

Although we do not like to admit it, some of us relax a bit when our bosses are away. The same productivity and fastidiousness that we display in the presence of our supervisors is often missing when they are on vacation. Perhaps we come to work a little bit later, take longer breaks, and leave a few minutes earlier. With no one looking over our shoulders, we may not put forth the same effort that we normally would.

Paul cautions us against such languid behavior. Even though Christ has gone away, He promises that He will return, and we do not want to be caught goofing off when He does. His coming will be like a thief in the night. Thus, while other people indulge their passions and proclivities, we must be alert and ready to respond to the sound of His voice. We must not seek to please our flesh, but we must seek to walk in the Spirit so that we do not fulfill the lust of our flesh (Galatians 5:16). If we do this, then we will be found ready to receive the coming of the Lord.

MESSAGE POINTS

Message Point 1: Comfort during grief (1 Thessalonians 4:13–18)

Paul begins our text with reassurance for the church regarding Christians who have died. Death for Christians does not represent the end, but it represents a transition to a new and glorious beginning. We do not grieve over those who have passed from death into life in the same way that nonbelievers grieve over the dead (v. 13). Instead, although we grieve because we miss those whom God has called home, we also rejoice because we know that we will be joined together with them again when Christ returns.

As Paul declared elsewhere, to be absent from the body through death is to be present with God (2 Corinthians 5:8). When Christ returns, both the dead and the living will be caught up in the air to meet Christ, and they will live with Him forever (v. 18). For those of us who have lost loved ones, this should comfort us in the midst of our grief, and this hope should instigate the type of faithful and sacrificial living that will please the Lord.

Message Point 2: The Day of The Lord will come suddenly (1 Thessalonians 5:1–5)

Paul next warns the church about the day of the Lord that signifies the Second Coming of Jesus Christ. The day of the Lord will come when most people least expect it. While people are enjoying the fruits of their labor and forecasting imminent periods of economic and political peace, the Lord will come suddenly to destroy the works of darkness and gather His children together. We must not heed the voice of nonbelieving economists, theorists, and pundits who claim to know the future. While they can successfully make limited claims about world events, they cannot forecast the return of the Lord, an event that no one can predict (Matthew 24:36). While they invest totally in the treasures of this life, we invest in spiritual treasures. Our plans are contingent and provisional, meaning, we give greater priority to spiritual things, and we put our full trust in nothing that is natural or material.

Message Point 3: We should live in expectation of Christ's coming (1 Thessalonians 5:6–11)
Paul declares that we are not children of darkness but children of the light (v. 5). We should not live our lives by satiating our desires with all types of imaginable pleasures, like hedonists, but we should be alert and sober minded. This means we must live in expectation that at any moment Christ could return. Paul's words remind me of my wife, who frequently helps me remember to keep our house clean. She is aware that at any moment guests could arrive unannounced. If our house is not kept in order, they may be dissatisfied with a messy environment, and we would be unprepared for them to stay.

The same is true of our Christian lives. Jesus can come at any moment, and we do not want him to be dissatisfied with the condition of our lives. Our metaphorical houses need to be in order so we can become excited at His return, knowing that our eager anticipation will have finally been fulfilled by His glorious presence.

THAT'LL PREACH

Before Paul wrote to the church in Thessalonica, Jesus used a parable to explain the urgency and unexpected nature of His return. It reads this way: At that time the kingdom of heaven will be like ten virgins who took their lamps and went out to meet the bridegroom. Five of them were foolish and five were wise. The foolish ones took their lamps but did not take any oil with them. The wise ones, however, took oil in jars along with their lamps. 5 The bridegroom was a long time in coming, and they all became drowsy and fell asleep.

"At midnight the cry rang out: 'Here's the bridegroom! Come out to meet him!'

"Then all the virgins woke up and trimmed their lamps. 8 The foolish ones said to the wise, 'Give us some of your oil; our lamps are going out.'

"'No,' they replied, 'there may not be enough for both us and you. Instead, go to those who sell oil and buy some for yourselves.'

"But while they were on their way to buy the oil, the bridegroom arrived. The virgins who were ready went in with him to the wedding banquet. And the door was shut.

"Later the others also came. 'Lord, Lord,' they said, 'open the door for us!'

But he replied, 'Truly I tell you, I don't know you.'

Therefore keep watch, because you do not know the day or the hour. (Matthew 25–13, NIV)

CONCLUSION

The Christian life should not be an expectation of ease and comfort, although we will enjoy times of peace and prosperity. However, we must also live in the Spirit, praying, reading our Word, and preparing ourselves for Christ's return. We will meet Christ in one of two ways. Either we will die in Christ and meet Him after we pass from this life, or, if we are alive when He returns, we will be caught up to meet Him in the air. Either way, we do not know the day nor hour when we will meet Him face to face. Therefore, we must live each moment in expectation that Jesus will appear.

NOTES

Don't Be Deceived!

By Elder Aaron O. Howard

Lesson Theme	Unit Theme	Scripture
Hope Comes from God's Grace	Beyond the Present Time	2 Thessalonians 2:1–3, 9-17

INTRODUCTION

It is always easy to identify deception when others are involved but less so when we are the ones being deceived. Television news shows frequently report on instances of deception in showing how people are swindled out of their money by persuasive con artists. The people who have been bilked out of their life savings appear foolish and naïve, and we think of ourselves as more careful and discerning than they are. However, we forget that deception is only successful because it resembles the truth. People do not invest their money in schemes that are obviously fraudulent. Instead, con artists go to great lengths to gain people's trust, ensure their confidence, and allay their fears. It is only after they have presented an image of integrity and honesty that they can deceive people. If we do not pursue righteousness and godliness, we too can be deceived by forces that disguise themselves as truth.

We must realize as Christians that Satan's job is to deceive us. If Satan appeared to us as he is depicted on Halloween—in a red outfit with horns and a pitchfork—then it would be hard for him to deceive anyone. Instead, Satan disguises himself as an angel of light, and his servants disguise themselves as followers of righteousness (2 Corinthians 11:14–15). To escape deception, believers must hold fast to the Word of God and love the truth.

MESSAGE POINTS

Message Point 1: Deception Knows No Boundaries (2 Thessalonians 2:1–3)

At the time that Paul wrote this letter, false prophets were spreading a deceitful message. They were telling the people of God that the day of the Lord had already come and that they had missed it. Even more surprising is the extent to which the deceivers attempted to mimic the truth to get their message across. Paul warned the church at Thessalonica that the deceivers may have sent a message or letter that looked like it came from him.

As believers, we must understand that Satan's deception knows no boundaries and that he will do whatever he can to mimic and imitate the truth while propagating his lies. Just because something sounds good or looks good does not mean that it is good. The enemy will appeal to our intellect, emotions, and desire to be liked by others in order to seduce us and draw us away from Christ.

Message Point 2: We Must Love the Truth or Else Be Deceived (2 Thessalonians 2:9–11)

Paul warns the church that the lawless one will perform signs and wonders and display great power. In other words, the one who acts like he is sent by God before the return of Jesus will in fact be sent by Satan. However, he will do things that people will assume that only one sent by God can do. If we are to escape these attempts at deception, we must be lovers of the truth.

A person that loves the truth stands on the Word of the God even when God demands what seems unfair, harsh, or unrealistic. Many times people assume that God's word does not apply to our contemporary context because we face temptations in ways that did not exist during the biblical times. People try to excuse sexual sin by appealing to this type of logic. However, this is a faulty view of God's will. This understanding of God's Word does not love the truth but rather prefers to be free from obedience and submission to God's Word. Such a view leads people to succumb to the enemy's deception, and God allows them to be deluded because they reject His Word. Their rejection of the truth leads ultimately to their demise.

Message Point 3: We Escape Deception Through Faith (2 Thessalonians 2:13–15a)

God has poured out His grace on those of us who believe. We did not first choose Him, but He first chose us (John 15:16). God has ordained from the beginning that we would be saved, but our salvation must be lived out through a sanctified life that demonstrates faith in the truth (v. 13). As Christians, we can glorify God regardless of Satan's attempts to thwart our testimony. We do this by holding fast to the Word of God that is revealed in the Bible. It is Paul who declared that even if an angel from heaven preached a gospel different from what he had preached, then that angel was to be considered cursed (Galatians 1:8). Whether someone claims to come from God and works miracles, or whether a person devises some new intriguing doctrine that seems appealing, if that person says or does anything contrary to the Gospel, we must not follow after them.

THAT'LL PREACH

One of Aesop's many fable teaches us the fate of those determined to deceive others: A Dog and a Rooster, who were the best of friends, wished very much to see something of the world. So they decided to leave the farmyard and to set out into the world along the road that led to the woods... At nightfall the Rooster, looking for a place to roost, as was his custom, spied nearby a hollow tree that he thought would do very nicely for a night's lodging. The Dog could creep inside and the Rooster would fly up on one of the branches. So said, so done, and both slept very comfortably. With the first glimmer of dawn the Rooster awoke. For the moment he forgot just where he was...so standing on tip-toes he flapped his wings and crowed lustily. But instead of awakening the farmer, he awakened a Fox not far off in the wood. The Fox immediately had rosy visions of a very delicious breakfast. Hurrying to the tree where the Rooster was roosting, he said very politely:

"A hearty welcome to our woods, honored sir. I cannot tell you how glad I am to see you here. I am quite sure we shall become the closest of friends."

I feel highly flattered, kind sir," replied the Cock slyly. "If you will please go around to the door of my house at the foot of the tree, my porter will let you in."

The hungry but unsuspecting Fox, went around the tree as he was told, and in a twinkling the Dog had seized him. The moral of the story is: those who try to deceive may expect to be paid in their own coin.

Source: Aesop, *Aesop's Fables* (1867)

CONCLUSION

Paul ends with a prayer of comfort and strength for the believer. We should not fear the attacks of Satan that will come because Jesus is our comfort and guide no matter what the prevailing circumstances may be. We are to lean on Jesus, knowing we already have victory over the enemy. Jesus is able to present us blameless before the Lord (Colossians 1:22), and we must trust that He who began this work in us will complete it (Philippians 1:6). By keeping our faith in Christ and His Word, we will emerge victorious and triumphant over the enemy.

May 7, 2023

A Living Hope

By Dr. Moussa Coulibaly

Lesson Theme	Unit Theme	Scripture
A Living Hope	Beyond the Present Time	1 Peter 1:3–12

INTRODUCTION

A Christian perspective of life in a difficult environment, in the midst of trials, or while suffering is the hope generated from the Resurrection of Christ from the dead. This hope of the Christian lives by knowledge of an inheritance preserved for him or her by God. God also preserves the Christian in adverse circumstances with the view of life to come. This is the salvation that the prophets proclaimed in their day.

MESSAGE POINTS

Message Point 1: Living Hope– Source of Praise to God (vv. 3–5)

The living hope of Christians is made possible by God's mercy and is based on the Resurrection of Christ from the dead. It is received through a new birth in Jesus Christ. For this, we praise God (v. 3) because man has no contribution to it. It is a gracious gift. This hope longs for an unalterable inheritance kept in heaven for Christians (v. 4). Christians are therefore protected by God until they reach the time when they will be able to fully enjoy their salvation (v. 5).

Message Point 2: Living Hope– Subject of Joy During Trial Tmes (vv. 6–9)

Such a hope generates joy, even in the midst of suffering. One can bear suffering with the expectation of receiving the inheritance forever (v. 6). Suffering has a role of sanctification in the Christian life just as fire has a role in the refinement of gold. Endurance in times of suffering can produce good character that will result in praise when Jesus Christ comes back (v. 7). Unlike Peter, the recipients of his letter have not seen Jesus Christ during His earthly ministry. However, they love Jesus and believe in Him. This fills them with great joy as a result of the hope that they have (v. 8). Their great joy is a reward of their faith. The final goal of their faith will occur at the last days with the ultimate salvation of their souls (v. 9).

Message Point 3: Living Hope– Content of the Old Testament Prophecies

Salvation that Christians now enjoy was spoken by the prophets in the Old Testament after diligent examinations (v. 10). They sought information on prophecies concerning Christ's suffering, the circumstances around it, and the glories that would follow (v. 11). The beneficiaries were not the prophets but eventual Christians. This would include Peter's readers, who received the Gospel through the preaching of eyewitnesses guided by the Holy Spirit.

THAT'LL PREACH

In addition to the Old Testament prophecies, the Book of Psalms can also serve as a source of hope for believers. Consider keeping the following verses close to you, write them down and post them around your home, in your car, or somewhere visible at your workplace.

"No one who hopes in you will ever be put to shame." (Psalm 25:3)

"For you have been my hope, Sovereign Lord, my confidence since my youth. 6 From birth I have relied on you; you brought me forth from my mother's womb. I will ever praise you. 14 As for me, I will always have hope; I will praise you more and more." (Psalm 75:5–6, 14)

"Yes, my soul, find rest in God; my hope comes from him. 6 Truly he is my rock and my salvation; he is my fortress, I will not be shaken." (Psalm 62:5–6)

CONCLUSION

Christians are saved by God through the new birth. This new birth ushers in a living hope for the future completion of their salvation. This is a subject of great joy; though, while waiting for the full manifestation of their hope, Christians have to suffer through the trials of the world. The salvation had been proclaimed by the prophets of the Old Testament for the future beneficiaries who we know now to be Christians, or followers of Christ.

NOTES

Equipped with Hope

By Rev. Sharon D. Smith, J.D.

Lesson Theme	Unit Theme	Scripture
Equipped with Hope	Beyond the Present Time	2 Peter 1:3–15

INTRODUCTION

In 1 Peter 1:3, we are told that God through Christ Jesus has given believers a living hope. What then is the source of this hope? And because we are equipped with it, how then are we to live? The answers lie in exercising faith and understanding the fruit that is borne of it. Imagine faith as the strong root system of a tree that produces branches, limbs, and fruit that are a testimony to our relationship to God through the Lord Jesus Christ.

MESSAGE POINTS

Message Point 1: The Knowledge of God through God's Glory and Goodness (2 Peter 1:3–4)
Everything we need to live a godly life has been given to us. The writer characterizes these things as God's promises. Because of these promises, we have hope and strive toward, and eventually reach, a perfected nature in God.

Message Point 2: A Virtue List (vv. 5–7)
What is set out in this text is a virtue list, a device commonly found in the New Testament. It is used as a teaching tool from which the reader or hearer can memorize and easily recall. We find such lists, for example, in Galatians 5:22–23 that outlines the fruit of the Spirit; in James 3:17, which says, "the wisdom from on high is pure, peaceable ...;" and here, in verses 5 through 7.

The virtues listed here build upon each other atop a foundation of faith. The faith that comes from reliance upon the "precious and great" promises (v. 4) that God has given generates goodness in us. From this goodness comes knowledge. From knowledge comes self-control, which yields endurance. Endurance creates in us godliness, and from godliness springs mutual affection ("brotherly love"). Mutual affection brings about the primary virtue: love. These virtues are the "things" referred to in verse 4 that God has given the believer.

Message Point 3: The Purpose of the Virtues (vv. 8–11)
The believer is equipped with faith to build goodness, knowledge, self-control, endurance, godliness, mutual affection, and love for a purpose. It is to keep a person from being "ineffective and unfruitful." Believers are called to be effective witnesses and do work that bears fruit for the Lord. Keeping the virtues at the forefront shields us from the things that cause us to stumble while empowering us to withstand in times of trouble.

Message Point 4: The Testament of Peter (vv. 12–15)
The first chapter of 2 Peter is referred to as Peter's testament, which is the passing on of wisdom or the testimony of a person's life. Here, we see Peter's purpose in writing: "I intend to keep on reminding you of these things."

He wants the believers who have been in his care and whom he has taught to remember the truth that has come to them. In true allegiance to Deuteronomy 6:6–9, Peter intends to repeat his words as long as he lives (v. 13) so that even after his death, believers will remember (v. 15).

THAT'LL PREACH

The eleventh chapter of the Book of Hebrews offers various examples of heroes and heroines of faith. Their stories show us what great things can happen when we have faith, even if it is just the size of a mustard seed (Matthew 17:20; Luke 17:6).

"By faith Noah, when warned about things not yet seen, in holy fear built an ark to save his family. By his faith he condemned the world and became heir of the righteousness that is in keeping with faith. By faith Abraham, when called to go to a place he would later receive as his inheritance, obeyed and went, even though he did not know where he was going. By faith he made his home in the promised land like a stranger in a foreign country; he lived in tents, as did Isaac and Jacob, who were heirs with him of the same promise... even Sarah, who was past childbearing age, was enabled to bear children because she considered him faithful who had made the promise... By faith the people passed through the Red Sea as on dry land; but when the Egyptians tried to do so, they were drowned... And what more shall I say? I do not have time to tell about Gideon, Barak, Samson and Jephthah, about David and Samuel and the prophets, who through faith conquered kingdoms, administered justice, and gained what was promised." (Hebrews 11:7–9, 11, 29, 31–33a)

CONCLUSION

From this text, several questions arise. Although we have been equipped with hope, are we exhibiting faith? How are we exercising our faith? What does it look like to others? What does it teach our children, our families, and others who look to us as leaders, brothers and sisters, or fellow laborers in Christ? Are we living as people who are equipped with hope? What is the testament that we are writing by the way we live?

NOTES

May 21, 2023

Hope through Stewardship

By Rev. Sharon D. Smith, J.D.

Lesson Theme	Unit Theme	Scripture
Hope through Stewardship	Beyond the Present Time	1 Peter 4:1–11

INTRODUCTION

We are called to be good stewards of that which the Lord has entrusted to us. Stewardship involves more than money. It includes our time, our talents, our possessions, our relationships, all that we have, and all that we are. God is the true owner of all that we have and have been given. Believers are expected to be ever mindful of who they serve and the value of that has been placed in their hands. The Gospel of Jesus the Christ is a precious commodity. If we claim its grace, its salvation, and the name of Jesus, then we are to walk circumspectly.

MESSAGE POINTS

Message Point 1: Purpose in Suffering (vv. 1–2)

Just as Jesus suffered for our sakes, we ought to endure suffering for the sake of the Gospel. This suffering was a sacrifice. The text tells us that if we've suffered (sacrificed), we've been saved from the penalty of sin and we've put the lifestyle of sin behind us. That is not to say that we never commit a sin; it is to say that sin is not our way of life. Examples of the lifestyle of sin are given in the verses that follow.

Message Point 2: Vice List (v. 3)

The writer makes his point by using the rhetoric of the vice list. This is a teaching by example of what not to do: Don't live in licentiousness, passions, drunkenness, reveling, carousing, and lawless idolatry. The Voice, a translation of the New Testament, presents the verse as "losing yourselves in sex, in addictions and desires, in drinking and lawless idolatry, in giving your time and allegiance to things that are not godly." (2 Peter 4:3, The Voice). All of these behaviors demonstrate a lack of self-control and an unwillingness to sacrifice wants for the good of the Christian life. Contrast this list with the virtue list found in 2 Peter 1:5–7.

Message Point 3: The Behavior of the "Others" (vv. 4–6)

It should first be noted that the word translated here as "gentile" does not mean people who are not ethnically or culturally Jews. Many of the people of the church community to whom this letter was written were not Jews. The Greek term translated as "gentile" is used in the New Testament to denote one from a different nation or even one who functions in a different culture. Here, the "gentiles" are outsiders, or nonbelievers.

Those nonbelievers who participate in the activities described in verse 3 are surprised that the believers do not indulge with them and therefore malign them. But, says the writer, those nonbelievers will have to answer to the Supreme Judge for their behavior and their treatment of those who believe.

Message Point 4: Be Disciplined (v. 7)

The Christian life is to be characterized by discipline. That is in direct contrast to the life lived without self-control. Verse 7 concludes "for the sake of your prayers." This parallels 2 Peter 3:7, "so that nothing hinders your prayers." This is a reminder of what Jesus taught, saying that when we pray, we should come to God free from the burden of conflict or ill-will toward our brothers and sisters. Also, we pray to be forgiven of our sins in the same way that we are to forgive others.

Message Point 5: The Behavior of Believers– Virtues (vv. 8–10)

Verses 8 through 10 present a mini-virtue list of behaviors. Believers are to be hospitable without complaining and to use the gifts that have been received from God to serve others. Above all, believers are to have "constant love" for one another. This sentiment is paralleled in 2 Peter 1:7 with love as the culmination of the list of virtues. We note also that the second half of 1 Peter 4:8 is one of the most quoted (and misquoted) verses of the New Testament. The love that "covers a multitude of sins" is translated elsewhere as love that "makes up for many faults" (The Voice).

Message Point 6: How We Serve and a Benediction (v. 11)

How are believers to exercise stewardship? We are to speak and act so that God, not the believer, is glorified. To emphasize the point, the passage concludes with a benediction: "To him (God) belong the glory and the power forever and ever." Amen.

THAT'LL PREACH

"IAM3," or "I am 3rd" is a top pillar of the Indiana Wesleyan University men's basketball team. The team's blog site describes it as "Building a team of 3rd in a culture of 1st." Head Coach Greg Tonagel and his coaching staff consistently remind the team that they are third. The concept is simple: it's God first, others second, yourself third.

From the beginning of the recruiting process, coaches tell prospective students what the team is about. While many are receptive, some are not. And that's okay. Players know the team is one that will pursue Jesus and love people. The team spends significant time praying, dreaming and seeking God together–even ministering locally through various avenues and going on regular mission trips to communicate the gospel.

Source: "Giving God Your All," Wesleyan Life Magazine, Fall 2017

CONCLUSION

There is the great temptation, especially in today's technology-driven society to compromise our standards, to "go along to get along." Everything is readily available and information, good and bad, is instantaneously accessible and presented. Movements and fads have arisen all around us. We are encouraged by the world around us to join in and indulge and even overindulge. But Peter urges us to live our lives "so that God may be glorified in all things" (v. 11). In our stewardship, we should always remember the commercial tag line of the Kosher meat producer Hebrew National® : "We answer to a higher authority."

NOTES

The Day of The Lord Is Coming

By Elder Aaron O. Howard

Lesson Theme	Unit Theme	Scripture
Hope in the Day of the Lord	Beyond the Present Time	2 Peter 3:1–15a

INTRODUCTION

For approximately 2,000 years, the church has been patiently waiting for the return of Jesus Christ. He promised that He would come again (Mark 14:26, Acts 1:11), but as the years continue to pass, the temptation to doubt Jesus arises. Instead of heeding the words of Christ, we may be tempted to adopt the views of scientists and researchers who believe that in a half billion years, all plant and animal life will cease due to the expanding heat of the sun. Presumably, as the sun burns itself out, the earth will wither away and be engulfed by the sun's heat. Scientists expect this process to be completed 7 billion years from now. Such a prediction neglects God's role in redeeming creation by refusing to acknowledge the day of God's judgment and God's creation of a new heaven and earth. Peter reminds Christians to live with urgency through Godly living and obedience by maintaining faith in the Word of God.

MESSAGE POINTS

Message Point 1: The Word of God is Trustworthy (2 Peter 3:1–7)

The author predicts that people will scoff at Christians for believing that Jesus is coming again after so many years have elapsed. This chapter was probably written within 30 years after the death and Resurrection of Jesus. Yet Peter, through the Holy Spirit, identifies the responses of later unbelievers who, not seeing any evidence of Christ's coming, claim that Christians have been duped.

Peter, however, refers to creation itself as evidence that the Word of God is sure. Just as God destroyed all life on earth through the flood, He will also do so again through fire. We are reminded that the only reason the heavens and earth still exist is because the Word of God sustains them until they will be destroyed on the Day of Judgment. The continued existence of the universe is evidence that the Word of God is sure because God created the universe by his Word, and we need only look at creation to be reminded that God's Word can be trusted.

Message Point 2: The Word of God is Not Constrained by Time (2 Peter 3:8–10)

With God, one day is like 1,000 years, and 1,000 years is like one day (v. 8). This means that God does not view time in the same way that we do. One thousand years may pass, but in God's eyes, that may be considered a brief period of time. Or, one day may pass by, but in God's eyes, that can be considered a long length of time. This is because God transcends time. God does not live in linear time as we do, and that is why He does not age or die. He is immune to the effects of time, and time is simply something He utilizes to fulfill His purposes.

Therefore, the coming of the Lord has not occurred because God is exercising patience, allowing people to repent and turn from their sins (v. 9). God is using time to maximize the number of people who will be saved. When the day of the Lord finally comes, it will come suddenly and without warning, and the opportunity for salvation will cease (v. 10).

Message Point 3: The Word of God Will Be Fulfilled (2 Peter 3:11–15a)
Because we know that the day of the Lord will be a terrible day in which the heavens and earth will be destroyed by fire, we must be found doing the will of God lest we be caught by this day unaware. We want to be ready to go with the Lord when He comes. The author admonishes us to be diligent in obeying God's Word by giving our attention to Godliness and holy living. Contrary to the world—which will be afraid and overcome by fear—we look for and anticipate the day of the Lord because we know that it will introduce the creation of a new heaven and earth in which we will dwell with the Lord forever (vv. 12–13).

THAT'LL PREACH

Consider the words of this poem from Naomi Thevenin, written for Power Poetry's Annual Emerging Poets Slam in 2017, which echo those of Peter in this passage:

"Cause a life without Jesus, / is like people trying to seize us. / Its horrible and boring / but Jesus is quite restoring. / I cant wait for the day, / that he picks up his children, / and takes them home, / and there are / no more stumbling stones. / Peace at last, no more fighting, / wars will be gone, families uniting. / To see the streets of gold, / in front of me, / will be like a lasting gift, / forever to see. / To see Jesus himself, / be the most delight, / see the smile on his face, / when i see him in the light. / To see heaven, / more beautiful than i imagined, / to see the angels, / and see their lights flashing. / Heaven is the place with no pain and suffering, / but down below us there is so much rustling. / I tell you today, / to start to believe, / because Jesus himself is coming, / he is ready to recieve."

CONCLUSION

We need not be consumed with the prognostications of scientists regarding the end of the world. Whether Jesus returns in our lifetime or thousands of years from now, we should live each day in expectancy and anticipation of His coming. We are to proclaim His Word to the lost so that they will turn from their sins and be saved. We should realize that God's patience means that He is extending the invitation of salvation to all who do not believe. The church's task is to actively witness to the truth of God's Word through obedience, proclamation of God's Word, and loving service. Jesus is coming again, and we must be ready for His return.

NOTES

June 4, 2023

Holy, Holy, Holy

By Dr. Ronald C. Potter

Lesson Theme	Unit Theme	Scripture
Holy, Holy, Holy	God's People Worship	Isaiah 6:1–8

INTRODUCTION

Many of us as Christians desire to do great things for God. We sincerely desire to be God's mouthpieces and instruments within a morally corrupt and spiritually fallen world. The 8th-century prophet Isaiah was motivated by the same desire. However, before Isaiah could answer the call to participate in the mission of God, there were some prerequisites for ministry that first had to be met. Isaiah's vision highlights these dimensions.

MESSAGE POINTS

Message Point 1: God's Majestic Holiness (Isaiah 6:1–4)

In Isaiah's vision, the redemptive and transformative mission of God is based upon the grander, almightiness, and holiness of God Himself. In the vision, Isaiah stands in awe of the greatness, power, and utter holiness of almighty God. Of all the divine attributes, however, it is the holiness of God that is paramount! The throne, the attending seraphs or angels, and the threefold chorus of "holy" all stress God's holiness, which includes both transcendence and righteousness. Isaiah envisions God as ultimately glorious! God's glory is His holiness, His separateness from all else, and His otherness. In light of this "big-God" vision, Isaiah feels acutely his finitude as well as his sinfulness.

Message Point 2: Confession of Sin (v. 5)

The brilliance of God's holiness reflects Isaiah's actual condition of unworthiness. In the radiance of God's holiness, Isaiah sees himself for what he really is: lost (ESV), ruined (NIV), and destroyed (NLT). Isaiah identifies himself with the uncleanliness of his people. In neither case is that uncleanliness simply ritualistic. It is moral! Isaiah and his people stand guilty before a holy God! This condition is not simply attributed to sinful acts. Isaiah and the people of Judah suffer from an internal state of uncleanliness.

In this vision, Isaiah finds himself in a dilemma that he cannot fix. He stands before a holy God guilty and unclean, and there is nothing he can do!

Message Point 3: Cleansing and Commissioning (vv. 6–8)

Although the actual word "grace" is not used in this section, what Isaiah experiences is a result of sheer grace! One of the seraphs takes a live coal from the altar and places it on Isaiah's lips saying: "Your guilt is taken away, and your sin atoned for" (v. 7b, NIV). Isaiah is cleansed, not by his own efforts, but purely by the grace of God. God has made provision not only for Isaiah's sinful condition but for all of Judah. This entire scene is actually a preview of God's provision for human sin through the finished work of Christ on the Cross 700 years later. The prophet Isaiah, who earlier confessed to be a man of "unclean lips," is now prepared to become God's mouthpiece. He readily answers the call: "Here am I, send me!"

THAT'LL PREACH

Let us consider how Jesus engaged with the Pharisees regarding internal cleanliness and what it means to be holy. Notice how he also references the prophet Isaiah:

> *"The Pharisees and some of the teachers of the law who had come from Jerusalem gathered around Jesus and saw some of his disciples eating food with hands that were defiled, that is, unwashed. (The Pharisees and all the Jews do not eat unless they give their hands a ceremonial washing, holding to the tradition of the elders. When they come from the marketplace they do not eat unless they wash. And they observe many other traditions, such as the washing of cups, pitchers and kettles.*
>
> *So the Pharisees and teachers of the law asked Jesus, "Why don't your disciples live according to the tradition of the elders instead of eating their food with defiled hands?"*
>
> *He replied, "Isaiah was right when he prophesied about you hypocrites; as it is written:*
>
> *'These people honor me with their lips,*
> *but their hearts are far from me.*
> *They worship me in vain;*
> *their teachings are merely human rules.'*
>
> *You have let go of the commands of God and are holding on to human traditions"...He went on: "What comes out of a person is what defiles them. For from within, out of men's hearts, come evil thoughts, sexual immorality, theft, murder, adultery, greed, malice, deceit, lewdness, envy, slander, arrogance and folly. All these evils come from inside and make a man 'unclean'"* (Mark 7:1–8, 20–23, NIV).

CONCLUSION

God calls us to be a holy people (1 Peter 1:15). Our holiness, however, is made possible by: 1) experiencing the grander and magnitude of God's own holiness; 2) seeing ourselves as we really are in light of God's holiness: lost, ruined, guilty, and unclean; 3) accepting God's provision for our sinful condition through the atoning work of Christ on the Cross; and 4) being receptive to answer God's call to witness in thought, word, and deed to His mission of restoration and salvation of our fallen world.

NOTES

Give Thanks

By Dr. Ronald C. Potter

Lesson Theme	Unit Theme	Scripture
Give Thanks	God's People Worship	Isaiah 12

INTRODUCTION

Throughout the drama of Scripture, God's people continually express gratitude and thanksgiving for all that God has done. In the 12th chapter of Isaiah, God's people are especially thankful for the "second exodus" that He will accomplish on their behalf. More importantly, however, the people are thankful for the messianic gift that they will receive: God Himself! This was God's promise to Israel. This is God's promise to us today.

MESSAGE POINTS

Message Point 1: Praise for God's Mitigated Anger (v. 1)

Praise for God's mitigated anger (v. 1)—God's judgment fell on Judah in the form of captivity to a foreign power because of its flagrant and perennial disobedience. Now, however, God's covenantal love (Heb., hesed) is again demonstrated toward His people by the promise of return to their homeland. God's anger is not only mitigated, or lessened, but nullified altogether. God is thanked for His forgiving love!

Message Point 2: Praise for God's Salvation (vv. 2–3)

In Revelation 7:10, a great multitude cried out, "Salvation belongs to our God," (NIV). Salvation is always a divinely initiated and achieved project. Humans are recipients of God's salvation. In this song of praise and thanksgiving, God's people are ever mindful that their coming "salvation-deliverance" from captivity is based on divine grace and mercy. What is more telling, however, is that the people recognize that salvation-deliverance is not simply an event but exists in the form of a person, "surely God is my salvation" (v. 2; NIV).

Message Point 3: Sharing Our Gratitude With Others (vv. 4–6)

The peoples' salvation-deliverance from captivity must be told to others. The salvation which was so graciously bestowed upon Judah by God is not something to keep quite about. The nations must be told about the gracious and liberating acts of Israel's God. Once again, however, emphasis is placed not simply upon the liberating activity of God as the liberating person of God. "Sing to the Lord, for he has done glorious things; let this be known to all the world." (v. 5, NIV).

THAT'LL PREACH

Consider the following quotes on gratitude:

"Be thankful for what you have; you'll end up having more. If you concentrate on what you don't have, you will never, ever have enough."
—Oprah Winfrey

"For me, every hour is grace. And I feel gratitude in my heart each time I can meet someone and look at his or her smile."
—Elie Wiesel, Holocaust survivor

"When eating fruit, remember the one who planted the tree."
—Vietnamese Proverb

"'Thank you' is the best prayer that anyone could say."
—Alice Walker

"Joy is the simplest form of gratitude."
—Karl Barth

CONCLUSION

Like the people of Judah, God's people today are urged to express our praise for what God has done in our lives. Our thanksgiving, however, must always focus upon the One who has so graciously saved and delivered us from bondage. Like the demon-possessed man who was healed and delivered, we are commissioned by Jesus to "Go home to (our) families and tell them how much the Lord has done for [us], and how he has had mercy on (us)" (Mark 5:19, NIV).

NOTES

Meaningless Worship

By Rev. Cheryl Price, Ph.D.

Lesson Theme	Unit Theme	Scripture
Meaningless Worship	God's People Worship	Isaiah 29:9–16a

INTRODUCTION

In this passage, the writer draws a connection between disobedience and false or insincere worship. The writer emphasizes the danger of not applying the Word of God to one's time and situation. It touches the apathy of the people, the prophets, and the nation of Israel (vv. 9–10); cynicism about the relevance of the prophetic word for their time (vv. 11–12); formal religion characterized by hypocrisy (vv. 13–14); and dependence on human scheming rather than the movement of God. The text also underscores the folly of assuming that deeds or deep inner motivations can be hidden from God (vv. 15–16).

We are reminded that God's chastisement does come, even though we often refuse to believe that we have to pay the consequences for sin. What are some consequences that you have had to pay for your sin?

MESSAGE POINTS

Message Point 1: Israel's Apathy (vv. 9–10)

Again, the people of Israel were not responsive or obedient to God's Word. The lack of response by the people reflects on the prophets as well. How did the prophets respond to such an uncaring attitude from the people? How do you respond when you keep God's Word to do what is righteous or encourage another to speak up to make changes in his or her life? Instead, the people of Israel continued to practice and live life their way. Their self-induced blindness became a way of life that would keep them from seeing or hearing how they were dishonoring God, themselves, and their nation.

How blind can we become when we only want things done our way, regardless of who or what else it affects, including our relationship with God? Why do we prefer to choose opportunities and relationships that keep us away from God and covered in darkness?

Message Point 2: Cynicism About the Prophetic Word (vv. 11–12)

Although God provided the land for the people, Jerusalem would be captured because the people were not open to God's Word. In fact, verses 11 through 12 are references to how closed they were to whatever the prophet said. Regardless of whether they could read or not, their minds and hearts were closed to digesting the message given to the prophet from the Lord. Their hearts had become hardened.

When does the church turn a closed ear to God's Word?

Message Point 3: Hypocrisy (vv. 13–14)

Unfortunately, the Israelites did not worship God with joyous hearts. They worshipped God in a routine manner from mundane hearts. Their worship was based on "we've done it this way for years" rather than a true or real desire to worship God. Words of praise and honor were devoid of sincere admiration and respect. The outward expression of the "religious" worshipers did not match their empty inner thoughts and feelings. The people were faking, as hypocrites who looked like worshipers, and did not really care to give all He is due and then some. How could they challenge their Creator and not show genuine care for God? Instead, they acted as if they did not need Him.

God did not like, and still does not like, us to practice the long and tried tradition of hypocrisy. Why do you think hypocrisy is a problem among Christians, and how can the Church stop perpetuating this?

Message Point 4: Keeping Secrets from God (vv. 15–16)

It is such a silly notion, but some of the Israelites thought they could hide from God. They believed He would not know their inner ambitions, heart's delights, or wants. The plots and plans they developed were not hidden. In fact, God let it be known that their undercover activity had been exposed. They did not understand that God gave them the ability to think and choose how to develop and live out their thoughts and desires. Yet, they would rather "hide" from God in the way that an ostrich might stick its head in the sand, thinking it's hiding but is completely visible. Hiding from God was not an option then, and it is not an option today. The earth and its inhabitants belong to God. No one can hide from God.

THAT'LL PREACH

Jesus also had a lot to say considering religious hypocrites:

"Woe to you, teachers of the law and Pharisees, you hypocrites! You give a tenth of your spices—mint, dill and cumin. But you have neglected the more important matters of the law—justice, mercy and faithfulness. You should have practiced the latter, without neglecting the former. You blind guides! You strain out a gnat but swallow a camel.

"Woe to you, teachers of the law and Pharisees, you hypocrites! You clean the outside of the cup and dish, but inside they are full of greed and self-indulgence. Blind Pharisee! First clean the inside of the cup and dish, and then the outside also will be clean.

"Woe to you, teachers of the law and Pharisees, you hypocrites! You are like whitewashed tombs, which look beautiful on the outside but on the inside are full of the bones of the dead and everything unclean. In the same way, on the outside you appear to people as righteous but on the inside you are full of hypocrisy and wickedness." (Matt. 23:23–28)

CONCLUSION

Have you ever tried to hide from God or think that if you don't speak it, then God won't do something about your secret?

NOTES

___

___

___

___

June 25, 2023

The Glorious New Creation

By Dr. Vincent Bacote

Lesson Theme	Unit Theme	Scripture
The Glorious New Creation	God's People Worship	Isaiah 65:17–21, 23–25

INTRODUCTION

Where do you look for hope? When we as Christians look around and see signs that say "all is not well," where do we turn to find out how this grand story of history will end? Today's text shows us that God made a great promise to us long ago.

MESSAGE POINTS

Message Point 1: The Promise of Life in the New World (vv. 17–19)

- God is going to renew His creation; it will be so transformed that it will truly be a new heaven and earth.
- The new world will be a place of great joy, and sorrows will be forgotten.
- This is cause for great celebration for those who have been living in exile and under the harm of empire.
- We can begin rejoicing now because of God's sure promise of the new world.
- Eternal life will change our perspective. We will think those who mark a century in years are only infants.
- Jerusalem will be the great holy city where we will live in security and feast on the delights of the land.

Message Point 2: Abundance of Life (vv. 20–21)

- These verses promise security and stability in the form of old age and a dwelling that also includes food to eat.
- Imperial violence threatens both of these aspects leading to premature death and food insecurity.
- God's vision of justice includes all aspects of life and promotes thriving rather than just surviving.

Message Point 3: The Promise of a Peace We Cannot Now Imagine (vv. 23–25)

- God's people will do work that bears great fruit. Our labors will lead to great flourishing.
- God's people will have an intimate relationship: There will be such closeness between God and His people that prayers will be immediately answered.
- The reverse of the curse: There will be no more violence between animals and no more enmity between people.
- Peace will endure forever: This will be God's holy world, where shalom is the "new normal."

THAT'LL PREACH

I want to revisit verse 25 for a moment. A popular category among viral videos is that of unlikely animal friendships. On National Geographic's YouTube channel there is a 45–minute video of the relationship between a chicken and a chihuahua. Some are even more unlikely like a pitbull and a parrot. These videos make us laugh and smile, but if you're like me, under the surface I worry that these friendships could take a turn for the worst. This is what makes the promise of peace in this passage even more amazing. God even cares about the animals and gives us a glimpse of the peace promised to God's people and all creation.

CONCLUSION

God tells us that history is going somewhere. Do we already give God praise and rejoice because of His sure promise? If anyone should live with hope, it should be God's people because God has given us inside information that tells us the end of the story. Let's show the world how we live in hope: When distress comes our way, we can admit that tough times are in the present but we also know that tough times are temporary. God holds the future, and when His promise arrives, peace, blessing, and wholeness will exist forever. Take the long view and live with rejoicing in our sure hope.

NOTES

July 2, 2023

Joyful Worship Restored

By Dr. Richard Gray

Lesson Theme	Unit Theme	Scripture
Joyful Worship Restored	God's People Worship	Ezra 3:1–7

INTRODUCTION

Within the Old Testament, the concept of God dwelling within the feeble bodies of humanity was extremely rare, if not perceived as heretical. For the most part, God dwelled among His people and within physical constructions. Thus, He had His own Temple, a place of worship and reverence. Ezra catalogues the restoration of that place.

MESSAGE POINTS

Message Point 1: Unity Among the People (v. 1)

- Unity was created and nurtured among the people of Israel. They moved as "one man."
- Though they had each settled in their respective towns, there was a central location for them to unite around.
- It is imperative for the people of God to have a place to meet together (Hebrews 10:25).

Message Point 2: Somebody Has to Step Up (vv. 2-3)

- Israel's religious and political authority was represented in Jeshua and Zerubbabel.
- The building of the altar of the Lord was initiated.
- Fear among the people of Israel was incited by threatening groups.
- The people of Israel turned to worship as a way of pleasing their God and seeking His protection.

Message Point 3: Staying True to the Word (vv. 4-5)

- The people returned to the Word of God for guidance.
- The Feast of Booths was initiated once again.
- The primary sacrifice of the burnt offering was displayed in conjunction with the freewill offering.

Message Point 4: Praise in Advance (v. 6)

- The people understood the purpose of the place they were building.
- Sometimes we have to step out in faith and do the thing we have been called to, even if we cannot see the tanigble results just yet.

Message Point 5: Know Your Neighbors (v. 7)

- Non-Israelite people aided in the construction of the Temple of God.
- This was practiced by King David and Solomon as well (1 Chronicles 22:2; 1 Kings 9:20–21).
- Help can come from the most unlikely places; it benefits you to know your neighbors and their gifts.

THAT'LL PREACH

There are several Scriptures that talk about construction, both in a physical and spiritual sense:

"The house which I am about to build will be great, for greater is our God than all the gods."
–2 Chronicles 2:5

"you also, as living stones, are being built up as a spiritual house for a holy priesthood, to offer up spiritual sacrifices acceptable to God through Jesus Christ."
–1 Peter 2:5

"For we are God's fellow workers; you are God's field, God's building."
–1 Corinthians 3:9

"For every house is built by someone, but the builder of all things is God."
–Hebrews 3:4

"For we know that if the earthly tent which is our house is torn down, we have a building from God, a house not made with hands, eternal in the heavens."
–2 Corinthians 5:1

CONCLUSION

God desires a place to worship—whether this place is within a human made construction of material or from within the very beating heart of humanity. Regardless, we must prepare ourselves to make room for Him in our lives, giving thanks and praise for His perfect love.

NOTES

Temple Restored

By Matthew C. Jones

Lesson Theme	Unit Theme	Scripture
Temple Restored	God's People Worship	Ezra 3:8–13

INTRODUCTION

God never promised us that His work would be easy. Thankfully, God has promised us His supply and victory in the work He has ordained. In Ezra 3, we see the work of God in tasking His people to rebuild the Temple. This was a historic and tremendous moment for the people of God to have the Temple restored. Yet hardship came as many in the community did not acknowledge the blessing at hand. As Christians, it reminds us of the blessing of the Father in sending His Son, who was also not acknowledged as the temple of God (Matthew 26:61), the actual presence of God among His people. By the grace of God in the mighty regenerating work of the Spirit, we have come to acknowledge Him and be restored in the gospel of Jesus, who works through us to extend His restorative work in the nations of the world.

MESSAGE POINTS

The Work of God in Restoring the Temple (Ezra 3:8–13)

At this point in the history of redemption, the people of God were longing for restoration. They had just finished many years of harsh exile in Babylon. In this context of despair, we read about God, who was faithful to deliver His people from exile and intentional in giving them a work in restoring not only their homeland, but also the Temple. The presence of the Temple was crucial theologically and politically, as it was the dwelling place of God where sacrifice was made and where the national symbol of God's sovereignty was known.

Message Point 1: Faithful to Complete the Work of God (vv. 8–9)

As the exiles returned home, the people of God faced the task of rebuilding their city, homes, and most monumentally the Temple. Ezra 3 reveals the faithfulness of God in restoring the Temple as the worship center of His people. The completion of the new Temple was a landmark event after years of exile in Babylon.

Message Point 2: Worshipful in the Carrying Out of the Work of God (vv. 10–11a)

Given the gravity of returning home and having the Temple restored, the workers began to sing, "praising and giving thanks to the LORD, saying, 'For He is good, for His lovingkindness is upon Israel forever'" (v. 11, NASB). While work—especially construction—is tiring, the people found great joy in worshiping as they carried out this historic undertaking. The first Temple was the dream of the great King David (2 Samuel 7:1–3), which his son, the legendary King Solomon, brought to fruition (1 Kings 5–6). This first Temple was destroyed by the Babylonians in 587 B.C. at the demise of the kingdom of Judah (2 Kings 25:9, 13–18; Psalm 74:3–7). And now, in Ezra 3, we see the people restoring the temple and worshiping "according to the directions of King David of Israel" (v. 10), emphasizing the connection between this second temple and the worship conducted in the first. This was reason for great joy and celebration.

Message Point 3: Joyous Despite Complainers in the Work of God (vv. 11b–13)
In verse 11, we read about how "the people shouted with a great shout ... because the foundation of the house of the LORD was laid." This scene reflects the story of the dedication of the first temple found in 2 Chronicles 5:12. Only in this case, there were naysayers among the people. The passage mentions how "the old men who had seen the first temple" (v. 12) began "weeping" (v. 13). The word used for weeping in the original Hebrew text (bakah) connotes that these were not tears of sorrow per se, but tears of complaint. One scholar observes, "Those who had known the first temple considered its construction to be considerably meaner, which reflects the relative poverty of the post-exilic community." Poverty is a demeaning experience, but for these seniors to take their plight out on the younger generation (also living in poverty) only compounded the hardship of those seeking to fulfill the work of God.

THAT'LL PREACH

Though the sanctuary was dark and debris was strewn everywhere, the church members circled up, held hands, and cried out to God. "Turn Your eyes toward the New Testament Baptist Church, dear Lord," Pastor Noland prayed fervently. "O God, speak to the four corners of the earth. You have somebody somewhere and we need You to send them our way." How did God answer? "That's when He brought Samaritan's Purse to us," Pastor Nolan said. "I praise the Lord for His goodness." Nine months since Irma and then Hurricane Maria ravaged the Caribbean, Samaritan's Purse is responding with one of the largest reconstruction projects [they've] ever undertaken. In cooperation with local churches, [Samaritan's Purse] deployed teams to St. Martin, Barbuda, Dominica, and Puerto Rico to repair or rebuild up to 3,000 houses and over 100 churches.

Source: Samaritan's Purse, "Rebuilding the Caribbean After the Hurricanes," accessed April 6, 2022, https://www.samaritanspurse.org/article/rebuilding-the-caribbean-after-the-hurricanes/.

CONCLUSION

It can be very discouraging to work hard for the Lord with limited supply only to face opposition from His people. We expect to face opposition from the enemies of God, but often, it comes from those in our own family. Imagine working so hard for years to survive exile, watching friends and family die, feeling constant aches in your body from labor, and losing hope as you prayed for God to deliver you. Then, imagine the joy of returning home and rebuilding the temple of the God you cried out to, experiencing joy in His deliverance and over the fruit of your labor. Now, imagine your joy being dashed by complainers who remind you that your work is not as good as it could have been or as good as theirs was in the past. While this was a hard reality to face, the complaining could not silence the praises of the younger generation. This life will never be free from hardship and hurtful complaining, but this is no reason for us to stop praising, to give up on restoration, or to lose joy. After all, we walk in the power of the Gospel of our Lord Jesus, "who for the joy set before him endured the cross" (Hebrews 12:12). Let us praise Him as we seek to build His temple in this age, the church, knowing that restoration involves hard work and that ample joy is to be found in it as we glorify the God who is mighty to save and faithful to restore.

NOTES

Dedication of the Temple

By Matthew C. Jones

Lesson Theme	Unit Theme	Scripture
Dedication of the Temple	God's People Worship	Ezra 6:13–22

INTRODUCTION

(Ezra 5–6)

- The prophets Haggai and Zechariah say it is time to rebuild the temple (5:1–2).
- The permission to rebuild the temple is challenged by the enemies of God's people (5:3–6:12).

MESSAGE POINTS

Joy Over God's Glory in the Temple (Ezra 6:13–22)

Message Point 1: The DUTY of Rebuilding the Temple is Documented by Government Policy (v. 13).

- Though the people know that God is the One who made it all possible, the authorization and support of the Persian kings is notable.
- Though this was likely a political move to extend control over the region, God's people used it as an opportunity to stay true to what was required of them in the Law.
- Rebuilding the Temple was not only a great technical, political, and social endeavor, which signaled the rebuilding of God's Beloved Community after experiencing imperial violence and exile.

Message Point 2: The DEED of Rebuilding the Temple is Done by God's People (vv. 14–15).

- In the rebuilding of the Temple, everyone had a part to play, from the prophets to the elders to the politicians.
- The primary focus was a spiritual one, with the prophet reminding the people of what God had called them to.
- This spiritual awareness had to be paired with a political savvy to work with the imperial offices.
- Most importantly, there had to be people who were willing to put in the physical effort to make this happen. Though they are not named, they are still key to the narrative.

Message Point 3: The DELIGHT of Rebuilding the Temple is Displayed by Great Praise (vv. 16–22)

- In this context, great praise is shown in the form of religious practice as instructed from the Law of Moses. Propitiation is offered (vv. 16–17). Priests are ordained (v. 18). Passover is observed (vv. 19–22).

- Celebrating Passover and remembering how God had delivered their people from bondage in a foreign land must have felt extra special for the diasporic peoples who had a central place of worship again.
- Israelites who had been living in exile could rejoice not just in the building that had been constructed but in the opportunity to feel at home again in their social and religious expressions.

THAT'LL PREACH

Often when people move into a new home or apartment, they have a "housewarming." This phenomenon has nothing to do with the temperature in the dwelling, but provides an opportunity for friends and family of the new occupants to bless them. Blessings can come in the form of money or gifts like household decorations, appliances, and food. Some people also choose to have their new homes blessed by their faith community. The doorways may be anointed and prayers shared in the space to invite God's protection and presence in the space. Both housewarming parties and the dedication of the Temple were causes of great joy and celebration for God's people.

CONCLUSION

KNOW: Behold the glory of God in the joy of His people as seen in salvation history.

FEEL: Bask in the grace of Jesus Christ who is our propitiation, priest, and final Passover (1 Corinthians 5:7).

DO: Believe the Gospel sharing the Good News as God continues building His temple today (Ephesians 2:19–22).

NOTES

Fasting and Praying

By Matthew C. Jones

Lesson Theme	Unit Theme	Scripture
Fasting and Praying	God's People Worship	Ezra 8:21–23

INTRODUCTION

(Ezra 7–8)

- The king empowers more exiles to return to their homeland, Jerusalem, the city of God (Ezra 7).
- The people evacuate Babylon with God's resources and protection for the journey ahead (Ezra 8).

MESSAGE POINTS

The Journey Out of Exile (Ezra 8:21–23)

Message Point 1: Waiting for God's Response by the Riverside (v. 21)
Setting up camp by the river Ahava to seek God's face invokes several similar situations in Scripture. One way to respond might be like when the people of God needed protection when escaping from Egypt and God brought them across the Red Sea (Exodus 14:19–31). Or they might be invited to simply rest and trust by the water like the Psalmist says, "He leads me beside quiet waters..." (Psalm 23:2b). Ezra shows great prophetic discernment by selecting this location to seek God's face for protection and direction.

Message Point 2: The Exiles Consider the Protection and Provision of God for The Journey (vv. 21b–22).
Ezra requires of the community spiritual as well as physical preparations. Even with the well-guarded royal roads, a long journey was hazardous, especially when transporting silver and gold. Ezra's humility and trust indicate that God's power is ultimately greater than that of the Persian king.*

Message Point 3: The Exilic Camp Becomes a Worship Center (vv. 23)
Through the mortification of fasting and prayer, the people seek God's face and God responds positively. Even in the middle of a tough transition, we can pray and fast to seek God's guidance. And this text demonstrates that such seeking is best sought in community with common needs, goals, and desires.

***Source:** Tamara Cohn Eskenazi, notes on Ezra in *The New Oxford Annotated Bible*, New Revised Standard Version, fifth edition, 2010.

THAT'LL PREACH

The practice of fasting in this passage bookends the exilic experience of God's people. Consider the account of Daniel and the Hebrew boys who began their time in Babylon with a fast:

But Daniel resolved not to defile himself with the royal food and wine, and he asked the chief official for permission not to defile himself this way. Now God had caused the official to show favor and compassion to Daniel, but the official told Daniel, "I am afraid of my lord the king, who has assigned your food and drink. Why should he see you looking worse than the other young men your age? The king would then have my head because of you."

Daniel then said to the guard whom the chief official had appointed over Daniel, Hananiah, Mishael and Azariah, "Please test your servants for ten days: Give us nothing but vegetables to eat and water to drink. Then compare our appearance with that of the young men who eat the royal food, and treat your servants in accordance with what you see." So he agreed to this and tested them for ten days.

At the end of the ten days they looked healthier and better nourished than any of the young men who ate the royal food. So the guard took away their choice food and the wine they were to drink and gave them vegetables instead. (Daniel 1:8–16, NIV)

CONCLUSION

KNOW: Realize that when you pray (Matthew 6:7) and fast (v. 16) the Father God sees (v. 18).

FEEL: Repent and experience the Good News of the Gospel of Jesus Christ who rescues us from exile.

DO: Revel in times of prayer and fasting as you wait on the Lord to bring us to His promised land (John 14).

NOTES

Gifts for the Temple

By Matthew C. Jones

Lesson Theme	Unit Theme	Scripture
Gifts for the Temple	God's People Worship	Ezra 8:24–30

INTRODUCTION

(Ezra 7–8)

- The **people of God** are saved from exile in Babylon (Ezra 7).
- The **preparation for going** straight home to Jerusalem (Ezra 8)
    - Finding the proper families for rebuilding the community (vv. 15–20)
    - Fasting and prayer for renewing contrition (vv. 21–23)

MESSAGE POINTS

The Generosity of Saved People (Ezra 8:24–30)

Message Point 1: Ezra Selects Priests and Patriarchs as Leaders (v. 24)

Ezra's preparations further empower the clergy for ministry among the saved exiles. In this passage it appears to be a family affair. Communities need strong families to carry out the calling God has placed on them. We recognize that today's families might look different than those described in the text. But whether chosen or given, we are all part of God's family.

Message Point 2: Ezra Sets Aside an Offering for the House of God (vv. 25–29)

Ezra entrusts the leaders to guard this great treasure, which had been gifted by many people from different ranks and social classes. Even if you do not have a large monetary sum to offer to the work of the Lord, your gift is still precious! Leaders are entrusted to recognize, call out, and develop the gifts of those around them for the glory of God. Our virtuous living out of our gifts is, in fact, is "more precious than rubies" (Proverbs 3:15; 31:10).

Message Point 3: Ezra Sees the Selected Leaders with Offering in Hand (v. 30).

Headed to the Temple in Jerusalem, the priest and the Levites acted as representatives of the people in the representative space of the relationship between God and God's people. The holiness of the vessels comes from their dedication to the Lord, not because of who is holding them. Leaders would do well to remember the Source of all we have and are. The best thing we can do is bring our gifts to God and seek discernment of how to best use them.

THAT'LL PREACH

Allow me to insert a "Christmas in July" moment. The Three Wisemen also brought Jesus gifts to celebrate the birth of the King of Kings (Matthew 2:1–12). Even more so than the Temple, Jesus was the embodiment and materialization of God's presence among God's people. And while we might not always be in a situation to give monetary gifts to God's temple, we can still give offers the gifts we already have. Recall the lyrics of the famous Christmas carol, "Little Drummer Boy":

"Come, they told me...Our newborn King to see...Our finest gifts we bring...To lay before the King...Little Baby...I am a poor boy too...I have no gift to bring...That's fit to give our King...Shall I play for you...on my drum?

I played my drum for Him...I played my best for Him...Then He smiled at me...Me and my drum"

(Song by Harry Simeone and Katherine Kennicott Davis, 1941)

CONCLUSION

KNOW: Worldly possessions are given to us so that by the way we use and give them, we proclaim in our hearts and display to the world that God is our supreme treasure and not the things of the earth.

FEEL: Witness the gospel as the ultimate gift of God, Himself in Christ, that makes every possession we have an opportunity to feel Christ's worth in counting it all as loss for Him.

DO: Worship God generously and intentionally in your heart, acknowledging Him as the supreme gift. For where your treasure is, there also will be your heart (Matthew 6:21).

NOTES

The Festival of Booths

By Dr. Vincent Bacote

Lesson Theme	Unit Theme	Scripture
Festival of Booths	God's People Worship	Nehemiah 8:13–18

INTRODUCTION

God's people return from the exile and have to begin restoring what was lost. Today, we see the return of an ancient festival and much rejoicing.

MESSAGE POINTS

Message Point 1: The People Hear God's Word (v. 13)
The Leaders of the Israelites come to Ezra to learn about the law. The people were ready to hear God's Word again. "Nehemiah 8 signals the historic moment when the Torah...is publicly (re)introduced and receives communal sanction. Thus the ceremony in [this chapter] echoes Sinai as the receiving of God's teachings by the entire people, transforming them into 'the people of the Book'."*

Message Point 2: The People Learn About and Embrace Their Heritage (v. 14–16).
The people learn about God's words given through Moses. The people learn about the Festival of Booths. Booths are temporary shelters that remind them of when they were protected by God while in the wilderness on the way to the Promised Land. Upon learning about their heritage, the people immediately act. The Israelites go out and make temporary shelters. Temporary shelters spring up everywhere; the people are enthusiastic in their obedience to God's Word. What do we as a people need to urgently remember? There is much to celebrate in many-layered stories of our collective memory.

Message Point 3: The People Celebrate (vv. 17–18)
The Time of Exile ended; the time of celebration begins. The joy of celebration "that this chapter describes extend over several weeks...longer than any other celebration in the Bible."* The people gather to hear God's Word on the eighth day. The central focus of the celebration echoes Joshua's leadership into the Promised Land, leadership that was grounded in following the Word of God as given by Moses. Thankfully they had these written records to help shape their celebration. May we honor the written and oral stories of the Church mothers and fathers who instructed us in the ways of the Word. They knew this was the only way to live and overcome all of life's hardships, all while finding a reason to celebrate.

***Source:** Tamara Cohn Eskenazi, notes on Nehemiah, *The New Oxford Annotated Bible*, New Revised Standard Version, fifth edition, 2010.

THAT'LL PREACH

Establishing the Festival of Booths (Tabernacles)

"So beginning with the fifteenth day of the seventh month, after you have gathered the crops of the land, celebrate the festival to the Lord for seven days; the first day is a day of sabbath rest, and the eighth day also is a day of sabbath rest. On the first day you are to take branches from luxuriant trees—from palms, willows and other leafy trees—and rejoice before the Lord your God for seven days. Celebrate this as a festival to the Lord for seven days each year. This is to be a lasting ordinance for the generations to come; celebrate it in the seventh month. Live in temporary shelters for seven days: All native-born Israelites are to live in such shelters so your descendants will know that I had the Israelites live in temporary shelters when I brought them out of Egypt. I am the Lord your God." (Leviticus 23:39–43, NIV)

CONCLUSION

The Israelites went into exile because of continued infidelity to God. After returning from the exile, God's people were ready to recommit to God and obey His commands. This enthusiastic celebration marks a time of gratitude to God for His great faithfulness. Do we celebrate God's faithfulness like this when we recall how good He's been to us? We don't need to have an exile experience to incite us to praise Him. Our great salvation in Christ is reason enough to worship God with thanksgiving.

NOTES

August 13, 2023

Community of Confession

By Dr. Vincent Bacote

Lesson Theme	Unit Theme	Scripture
Community of Confession	God's People Worship	Nehemiah 9:2, 6–7, 9–10, 30–36

INTRODUCTION

"Confession is good for the soul." What happens when you hear God's Word? Does it make you tell the truth?

MESSAGE POINTS

Message Point 1: God's People Confess Sin (v. 2)

- The Israelites set themselves apart and admit their sin. Their confession is for their ancestors and for themselves.
- The separation from foreigners may seem strange, but it acknowledges the specific history and relationship between the Israelites and Yahweh.
- What collective harm has our community committed or been complicit in? What would collective confession and healing look like?

Message Point 2: God's People Confess the Truth About God (vv. 6–7)

- The Israelites proclaim God as Creator. We either honor or dishonor our Creator based on how we treat His creations, the Earth and her resources, as well as other people.
- The Israelites proclaim God as the Lord who chose Abraham. Who are the ancestors and heroes of faith in our community? How have we remembered their stories?

Message Point 3: God's people Confess that He Saved His People (vv. 9–10)

- The Israelites recall God's answer to the cries of suffering in Egypt.
- The Israelites recall God's rescue from the oppression of Pharaoh.
- We serve a notorious God. How has He made a name for Himself among us today?

Message Point 4: God's People Confess Their Covenant Infidelity (vv. 30–36).

- The Israelites thank God for His faithfulness and mercy because they were not destroyed by neighbors after many warnings.
- The Israelites confess God's faithfulness and their suffering for breaking covenant with the Lord.

- The Israelites lament their lingering slavery even as they return from exile.
- In what ways are we still in bondage today?

THAT'LL PREACH

In addition to the model of corporate confession exhibited in this passage, there are various Psalms of confession. These include Psalms 6, 32, 38, 51, 102, 130, and 143. Examine Psalm 130 for example:

Out of the depths I cry to you, Lord;
  Lord, hear my voice.
Let your ears be attentive
  to my cry for mercy.

If you, Lord, kept a record of sins,
  Lord, who could stand?
But with you there is forgiveness,
  so that we can, with reverence, serve you.

I wait for the Lord, my whole being waits,
  and in his word I put my hope.
I wait for the Lord
  more than watchmen wait for the morning,
  more than watchmen wait for the morning.

Israel, put your hope in the Lord,
  for with the Lord is unfailing love
  and with him is full redemption.
He himself will redeem Israel
  from all their sins.

CONCLUSION

God's people yesterday and today need to praise Him always and proclaim the truth about Him. But our proclamation cannot be limited to our verbal utterances. We must proclaim the truth with our daily practices. Confession is good for the soul. God is ever faithful, and we should honor Him with our undying fidelity.

NOTES

Dedication of the Wall

By Dr. Vincent Bacote

Lesson Theme	Unit Theme	Scripture
Dedication of the Wall	God's People Worship	Nehemiah 12:27–36, 38, 43

INTRODUCTION

What's the right way to worship God? Is there a special way to give God proper reverence while also praising Him? The dedication of the wall in Jerusalem gives us an example of celebratory worship to God.

MESSAGE POINTS

Message Point 1: Strike Up the Band! (vv. 27–29)

- The dedication begins with joyful songs and musical instruments.
- Joyful music: Worship is an offering to God in the words we sing and the way we play our instruments.
- Groups of singers and musicians were reunited from across different regions.
- The initiative to worship in response to all God has done comes from the community.

Message Point 2: Prepare yourself (vv. 30–36, 38)

- The priestly purification indicates a readiness for worship. Not only are you calling upon God's presence with your worship, you are setting the atmosphere for the whole community.
- The prelude to thanksgiving involved two choirs at the ready. They started marching in opposite directions and met in the middle. Sometimes we are resistant to new styles of worship. But if we meet in the middle and end up praising the same God, is not that what it is all about?
- The processional: following directives of King David. Again the practices of those who have gone before are key.

Message Point 3: Bring the Sacrifice of Praise (v. 43)

- The people bring offerings. Again the focus is not so much financial, but an offering of praise.
- All the people rejoice, even the children. "Through the praise of children and infants you have established a stronghold against your enemies, to silence the foe and the avenger." (Psalm 8:2)
- Unfettered praise: The neighbors knew God had brought joy to His people. What is our collective testimony?

THAT'LL PREACH

Invite the congregation to participate in a praise and worship song, paying close attention to how the lyrics invite the listeners to remember all that God has done for them and who God is, making God worthy to be praised. Consider the first verse and chorus of the classic Mary Mary song, "Shackles":

In the corners of my mind
I just can't seem to find a reason to believe
That I can break free
Cause you see I have been down for so long
Feel like the hope is gone
But as I lift my hands, I understand
That I should praise you through my circumstance

Take the shackles off my feet so I can dance
I just want to praise you
I just want to praise you
You broke the chains now I can lift my hands
And I'm gonna praise you
I'm gonna praise you

Written by Erica Atkins, Trecina Atkins, Warryn Campbell, Franne Golde, Dennis Lambert, Duane Hitchings
Produced by Warryn Campbell 2000

CONCLUSION

Do you worship with enthusiasm? Does God's provision, goodness, and faithfulness prompt you to bring a sacrifice of praise? There's certainly time for silent reflection in our worship, but God is honored when His people rejoice enthusiastically because of the great things He has done.

NOTES

August 27, 2023

Sabbath Reforms

By Dr. Vincent Bacote

Lesson Theme	Unit Theme	Scripture
Sabbath Reforms	God's People Worship	Nehemiah 13:15–22

INTRODUCTION

"Remember the Sabbath Day?" In the era of a 24-hour news cycle and the endless push to be successful and get ahead, what place is there for the Sabbath? Why should we care?

MESSAGE POINTS

Message Point 1: Business as Usual? (vv. 15–16)

- The Jewish people continue to work on the Sabbath.
- Merchants from Tyre enter the city and sell to the people on the Sabbath.
- Is it just another day like all the others?

Message Point 2: This Is a Warning! (vv. 17–18)

- Nehemiah rebukes the leaders.
- Nehemiah recounts the wrath of God that came in the past.
- Is this a case of amnesia?

Message Point 3: Time for Corrective Measures (vv. 19–21)

- Nehemiah closes the gates on the Sabbath.
- Nehemiah warns the merchants from Tyre.
- What does Nehemiah remember about the Sabbath?

Message Point 4: Turning to God (v. 22)

- The priesthood is called to purify themselves and as boundary-keepers for the sabbath. This reinforces the holiness of the entire city as dedicated to the Lord.
- Nehemiah's plea for God's for mercy shows that sometimes leaders can only lead a horse to water, but cannot force them to drink. It is up to the people to accept wise counsel.
- The God of mercy is also Lord of the Sabbath.
- How do you keep the Sabbath holy?

THAT'LL PREACH

Consider these three tips for keeping the Sabbath holy in our modern times:

1. Sleep Differently

Like those Snickers commercials, "You're not you when you're hungry," you're not you when you're tired. Our bodies are wired to sleep a third of our day. When the work of the week impinges on that rest, you need to embrace sleep. If you wake up to an alarm every day, don't set an alarm on the sabbath. Listen to your body. Wake up when your body wakes up. Take a nap. Start your sabbath evening by going to bed at a reasonable hour so you can get at least eight hours of sleep.

2. Put Away Your Screens

Put your smartphone in a sock drawer for 24 hours. Turn it off. Missing a dozen notifications has yet to kill anybody. At the very least, delete your social media apps for 24 hours. It takes about 30 seconds to re-install them the next day. Kill your electronic distractions, if only for one day a week.

You don't have to be present to everyone all the time. Your presence is more valuable to the people right in front of you. You may be surprised by what you find when you lift your eyes beyond your screen.

3. Make Something

Doodle in a sketch pad. Tend a garden. Work on a novel. Paint a picture. Create something with your hands. Don't do this out of obligation. This isn't about fixing up your house because it's on your to-do list. This is about the joy of creation because you are made in the image of the ultimate Creator.

Source: Peter White, "12 Practical Tips for Sabbath Keeping," The Sabbath Life, accessed April 6, 2022, https://www.thesabbathlife.com/sabbath/practical-tips-sabbath-keeping.

CONCLUSION

God made the Sabbath for us. Do we think God is keeping something from us if we disregard it? We should seek to honor God's commands and trust His provision for us instead of trying to establish our security by ourselves. Observing the Sabbath shows that we trust God and not ourselves or anyone else to take care of us. Nehemiah knew this and had to give his people a stern reminder.

NOTES

Our Marching Orders

By Dr. Vincent Bacote

Scripture

Matthew 28:16–20

INTRODUCTION

It is good for us to remember that the Lord we serve has given us the great opportunity and task to participate in His mission of spreading the Gospel. Jesus is our king: What are His orders for us?

MESSAGE POINTS

Message Point 1: The Appearance of the King (vv. 16–18a)

- The disciples gather and wait in anticipation for Jesus to appear and teach them.
- Some disciples worship and some doubt as He approaches.
- The resurrected Jesus comes near to His people.

Message Point 2: The Command of the King (vv. 18b–20a)

- Jesus declares His sovereign rule over everything.
- Jesus commands us to spread the Gospel to the world and to make disciples.
- Jesus commands us to teach and baptize under His authority.

Message Point 3: The Assurance of the King (v. 20)

- Jesus is with us always through the power of the Holy Spirit.
- Jesus will go with us as we obey the Great Commission to make disciples of all nations.
- Jesus' presence with us assures us that in the end, God will have the victory.

THAT'LL PREACH

When Christianity first began, it was a small crowd following Jesus who traveled throughout Galilee performing miracles and sharing the Good News. Through the working of the Holy Spirit, Christianity has become the largest religion in the world. Out of over 7 billion people in the world, 2.3 billion, or 30.9%, adhere to the Christian faith. Although this is a great milestone, there is an even greater challenge that our faith is facing. Namely, the Church of today seems to have turned a blind eye to those who have never heard of the Gospel. In fact, according to the Global Commissions Partners' website , 70% of evangelical Christians have never even been told about the 1.6 billion unevangelized people in the world. How are we supposed to take the Gospel to the unevangelized if we do not even know about them?

CONCLUSION

Today, we can recall that the King we serve is the One who has overcome the world and gives us the tremendous privilege of making disciples from every part of the world. What will you do today? Will you take the marching orders of your King and spread the Gospel? Let us not delay, and let us eagerly share this Good News with a dying world.

NOTES

Learning From Lent

By Matthew C. Jones

Scripture

Various texts

INTRODUCTION

- **What is Lent?**—Since ancient times (4th century), Christians have observed Lent as a time of repentance and remembrance over the work of Christ.
- **How long does it last?**—From Ash Wednesday to Easter, Lent lasts for a period of 40 days.
- **What does it entail?**—Spiritual disciplines of prayer, almsgiving, and self-denial are practiced as acts of worship unto the Lord during Lent.

MESSAGE POINTS

Biblical Theology of Lent

Message Point 1: The Number 40 in the Hebrew Bible

- Noah survived God's flood of 40 days and nights (Genesis 7:4).
- Moses spent 40 days on Mount Sinai with God (Exodus 24:18).
- Israel wandered in the desert for 40 years (Numbers 14:33).
- Elijah journeyed 40 days and nights to Mount Horeb (1 Kings 19:8).
- Jonah spoke of 40 days of judgment in Nineveh (Jonah 3:4).

Message Point 2: The Typology and Teaching of Jesus

- Jesus spends 40 days and nights in the wilderness facing temptation (Matthew 4:1–2; Mark 1:12–13; Luke 4:1–2).
- Jesus rebukes Satan by quoting the Hebrew Bible, specifically references about Israel's wilderness experience (Deuteronomy 6:13, 16; 8:3).
- Jesus replays Israel's 40 years in the wilderness, for just like Israel, He was tempted:
  - By hunger (Exodus 16:1–8)
  - To put God to the test (Exodus 17:1–3)
  - To idolatry (Exodus 32)
- Jesus regards fasting as a normal part of discipleship (Matthew 6:16).
- Jesus reprimands the exercise of spiritual disciplines for the notice of others (Matthew 6:16–17).

Message Point 3: The Theology of Self-Renunciation

- Israel's covenant with God involved built-in rituals of fasting for the community (Leviticus 16:29–31; 23:26–32; Numbers 29:7; Joel 1:14)
- Jesus called for His disciples to be marked by self-renunciation (Luke 9:23–26; Matthew 16:24–25; Mark 10:17–22) and fasting (Mark 9:14–29; Luke 9:37–42)
- The churches in Antioch and Galatia fasted in preparation for evangelical mission (Acts 13:1–3, 14:21–23).
- The concern of fasting is very practical and personal (1 Corinthians 7:5).
- The Christian life inevitably involves periods of suffering and includes fasting (2 Corinthians 6:4–10, 11:23–28)

THAT'LL PREACH

Dieting fads have come and gone throughout the years. Keto, low-carb, pescatarian, paleo, the list goes on and on. People often struggle maintaining diets and that can sometimes negatively impact their health. The call to fast for Lent is not meant to harm your body but to strengthen your spirit. Ask the Holy Spirit to help you discern the areas in which you can grow closer to God. What might you need to shift your attention away from in order to focus more on God? It can feel good to receive compliments for making an outward change in our appearance, but how much better would it be to have the "incorruptible beauty of a gentle and quiet spirit, which is very precious in the sight of God"(1 Peter 3:4).

CONCLUSION

The Delight of Lent

- Even in the midst of hardships, there is great delight in fasting (Daniel 9:2–3).
- Even in the midst of hunger, there is fullness in fasting by God's Word (Deuteronomy 8:2–3; Matthew 4:4).

The Danger of Lent

- Lent has no ability to confer grace (sacramentalism).
- Lent has nothing to convey in terms of righteousness (Pharisaism).

The Dream of Lent

- Self-denial accredits the One who gives us our strength: the Lord Jesus Christ.
- Lent anticipates the return of Jesus Christ (Matthew 9:14–15).

NOTES

Pursue Life with God

By Rev. Sylvester Warsaw, Jr., Outreach Pastor

Scripture

Psalm 37:1–11 (NKJV)

"Do not fret because of evildoers. Nor be envious of the workers of iniquity. For they shall soon be cut down like the grass, And wither as the green herb. Trust in the LORD, and do good; Dwell in the land, and feed on His faithfulness. Delight yourself also in the LORD, And He shall give you the desires of your heart. Commit your way to the LORD, Trust also in Him, And He shall bring it to pass. He shall bring forth your righteousness as the light, And your justice as the noonday. Rest in the LORD, and wait patiently for Him. Do not fret because of him who prospers in his way, Because of the man who brings wicked schemes to pass. Cease from anger, and forsake wrath; Do not fret—it only causes harm. For evildoers shall be cut off; But those who wait on the LORD, They shall inherit the earth. For yet a little while and the wicked shall be no more; Indeed, you will look carefully for his place. But it shall be no more. But the meek shall inherit the earth, And shall delight themselves in the abundance of peace."

INTRODUCTION

It is an honor to deliver today's commencement address to this year's graduating class. Today, it is my hope that you all are encouraged and challenged by that which God has given me to communicate to you as clearly as possible as you embark on a new phase in your young lives that God has given you.

MESSAGE POINTS

Message Point 1: Seek God's Face Daily and Be Yourself

First and foremost, I want you to know that God is no respecter of persons. Just because you are a Christian does not mean that you are not going to having challenges. The question is: How will you handle the challenges that you are going to encounter? The challenges of life are equally opportunistic; therefore, it matters not whether you are a Christian or a non-Christian. The Bible teaches us in Matthew 5:45 that "[God] makes His sun rise on the evil and on the good and sends rain on the just and on the unjust." Because of the truth of God's Word, we are responsible for the decisions we make. We cannot base our actions on what others do because, then, our actions become reactions. This is what verses 1 through 2 are telling us. We must take ownership of our decisions, not blaming anyone for the decisions we make. Being responsible and operating out of a value system speaks volumes of you as a person. Our value system should be built on having a personal relationship with God by seeking His face daily.

Message Point 2: God is the Foundation for True Success

I want the truth of verses 3 through 5 to soak in, so listen to the wisdom of these words from God again: "Trust in the LORD, and do good; Dwell in the land, and feed on His faithfulness. Delight yourself also in the LORD, And He shall give you the desires of your heart. Commit your way to the LORD, Trust also in Him, And He shall bring it to pass." There is a difference between worldly success and godly success. Worldly success is motivated by greed, whereas with godly success, the motivating factor is servant-leadership. Godly success is what God does in and through us when we trust Him, dwell in Him, delight in Him, and commit our way to Him. Godly success is not based on your station in life, your status, your address, or your bank account. Godly success is based on God using you to influence and make an impact on the lives of people He allows you to encounter in a way that glorifies and honors Him. We make the choice daily, whether we will serve God or chase after the idolatry of riches.

Message Point 3: Meekness Pays Off

When we recognize our need for and dependence on God, our position becomes one of humility and thankfulness. According to the standards of this world, these characteristics are signs of weakness. God has called His children to a higher standard of living than what this world order teaches. When we seek the face of God, He then teaches us His way, and we, as His children, can stand on the promises of His Word. Verse 7 tells us to "rest in the LORD, and wait patiently for Him." The command to rest and to wait is of great importance because it tells us that God is at work; He is working His will to help His children prosper. We can't serve God and try to get riches by any means necessary. When we can go to sleep at night with a clear conscience, thanking God for having the opportunity to serve Him by being a servant-leader, we can see that He will count it as righteous before Him and bring forth your righteousness as the light.

THAT'LL PREACH

"First generation college students are the first students in their family to go to college, and these students face different obstacles than their peers who come from generations of higher education. To add to that distinction, African American first generation students have even more obstacles solely based on their race [due to] institutionalized racism. The systems that have been set into place ... separates them from their peers and can ... deter these students from their studies. According to PNPI.ORG, among all undergraduate students, the U.S. Department of Education classified 41% of African American students to be first generation. In comparison, 25% of white and Asian students combined were determined to be first generation students, which is much less than that of African American students. College is about finding your passion, your tribe, and yourself. Making a way for yourself in college as an African American first generation student can be overwhelming. Look for your support, don't be afraid to ask for help, and use every resource available. This new journey is going to be what you make of it, so make it great."

Source: Currence, Thursday. "Black Voices: Black first generation college students share struggles, success stories." Indiana Daily Student (Bloomington), Novemeber 10, 2021. https://www.idsnews.com/article/2021/11/black-college-students-share-struggles-success-stories-us-dept-education.

CONCLUSION

There is a great big world with many challenges waiting for you. You have the choice over how you will address and meet those challenges. Many of you are without hope amid bleak opportunities because you're looking for someone to give you a job. Then there are those who see the opportunity to use what God has given them by trusting Him to bring about His Will in and through them for His glory and honor. Today, I call you to turn to God and trust Him with your future. Look to Him and not to the seductive idols in the world. He will honor your faithfulness to Him. Thank you for inviting me to address this graduating class. I pray that you heard a word from God speaking to your heart. He wants to give birth to something in your lives that will benefit the Church, our society, and you.

NOTES

God's Earthly Choice To Father His Son

By Rev. Sylvester Warsaw, Jr., Outreach Pastor

Scripture

Matthew 1:18–25, NKJV

"Now the birth of Jesus Christ was as follows: After His mother Mary was betrothed to Joseph, before they came together, she was found with child of the Holy Spirit. Then Joseph her husband, being a just man, and not wanting to make her a public example, was minded to put her away secretly. But while he thought about these things, behold, an angel of the Lord appeared to him in a dream, saying, 'Joseph, son of David, do not be afraid to take to you Mary your wife, for that which is conceived in her is of the Holy Spirit. And she will bring forth a Son, and you shall call His name JESUS, for He will save His people from their sins.' So all this was done that it might be fulfilled which was spoken by the Lord through the prophet, saying: 'Behold, the virgin shall be with child, and bear a Son, and they shall call His name Immanuel,' which is translated, 'God with us.' Then Joseph, being aroused from sleep, did as the angel of the Lord commanded him and took to him his wife, and did not know her till she had brought forth her firstborn Son. And he called His name JESUS."

INTRODUCTION

In this country, we hope that we marry for love. However, we know that people get married for various reasons. We may not be familiar with or understand cultural practices pertaining to pre-arranged marriages, but allow me to replay the events leading up to Joseph and Mary's wedding ceremony. Joseph and Mary are betrothed to each other, and the unthinkable happens! Mary, who is supposed to be a virgin, is pregnant, and Joseph knows he has not slept with her. This must have rocked Joseph's world in more than one way, considering the text says, "He was minded to put her away secretly." But there were other dynamics at work that Joseph was not aware of. God was taking notice of Joseph, and we could agree that God had chosen Joseph for a task that would change the course of history as humanity knew and understood it.

MESSAGE POINTS

Message Point 1: Joseph, a Just Man

When God saw Joseph, He saw a man who loved, worshiped, and revered Him. God saw a man of Godly character. The text in verse 19 says that Joseph was a "just man," a righteous man. This says a great deal about what God thought of Joseph. God also knew that Joseph would do right by Mary, regardless of what the circumstance appeared to be. God knew Joseph would rear Jesus with a godly heart. Joseph knew the importance of having a relationship with God the Father; therefore, Joseph's righteousness wasn't self-righteousness but godly. God knew Joseph's heart.

Message Point 2: Joseph's Obedience

Unlike many of us, Joseph didn't question God or throw out a fleece for proof of what the angel of the Lord had said to him in his dream (Judges 6:36–40). Often, God shows us what He's doing, but our lack of faith prevents Him from being glorified and honored in our lives. The text says in verse 24, "Then Joseph, being aroused from sleep, did as the angel of the Lord commanded him and took to him his wife." To be aroused suggests a sense of urgency. The angel of the Lord did not allow him to finish sleeping but woke him out of his sleep. This says it was a time for action, not sleeping. This tells you and I that when God shows us His plans for our lives, it's time to move, not sleep. Too many of us are sleeping when God is calling for action.

Message Point 3: Joseph's Love for God and Mary

Verse 25 says, "and [Joseph] did not know her till she had brought forth her firstborn Son." Their marriage was not consummated until after Jesus' birth. We, in our culture, put a larger premium on sex than we do love. The physical act of lovemaking is a powerful experience but only in a marriage between a man and a woman. Joseph did not seek his own pleasure but sought to please the Lord by honoring Mary who was with child, conceived by the Holy Spirit. Joseph realized that God was entrusting him to be a father to His only begotten Son, Jesus. This realization humbled Joseph. The Lord had chosen Joseph to do something no one else would ever do, and that was to be the earthly father of Jesus.

THAT'LL PREACH

Blended families have always been around, whether we like to talk about them or not. Because of different life experiences, some couples get together later in life after they already have children of their own. But what a blessing to see a family grow and a step-parent embrace a child that is not their own. It takes a special kind of love to be a bonus parent. Joseph shows an example of how you can love your partner AND their child. It might go against what society expects from such a situation, but Joseph gives a great example of someone who stepped up to the plate and made it work for the love of his family and the glory of God.

CONCLUSION

Children are a gift from God, and God expects us to give the children He has placed in our lives a Godly heritage. We have to invest in our children by imparting what God has given us to teach them. Our children must see us seeking the face of God. They must see us loving our wives as Christ loves the Church. Our children must know that we love them enough to be there for them. As fathers, we are called to serve our families, not for them to serve us as if we were some kind of earthly kings. Even though we won't be the earthly father of God's only begotten Son, the question remains: Does God see those same qualities in you and I that He saw in Joseph? Are you and I righteous in the eyes of God, or are we self-righteous in our own eyes? I pray that God is the One who sees our hearts and recognizes that we are living a righteous life before Him as stewards of our families.

NOTES